20 QUESTIONS ABOUT GOD

Peter Brown

Acknowledgements

I would like to express my deep gratitude to all the respondents whose thoughtful replies to my 20 Questions appear in this book. Thank you very much for allowing me to edit and publish your replies, and for revealing your selves through your answers.

I am indebted to Dr. Thomas Bartscherer, who was kind enough to take an interest in this work and write the splendid Foreword.

My thanks also to my parents and siblings, who have encouraged me to pursue classical studies, fostered my interest in the outdoors and the graphic arts, and allowed me to maintain a clear path in my tradition and a pluralistic view of others'.

Foreword

In the preface to his seminal work, *Varieties of Religious Experience,* William James writes of his "belief that a large acquaintance with particulars often makes us wiser than the possession of abstract formulas, however deep."[1] The book you have before you proceeds from a similar methodological conviction. Peter Brown has solicited responses to a carefully curated set of questions, and in what follows, he orders and presents them without imposing categories or interposing explanations. The questions themselves do evince certain concerns and inclinations—more on that below— but otherwise, we are presented with direct testimony from a diverse set of respondents to a set of questions about their own experience of and with religion. The wisdom gained, for author and reader, derives both from the richness of the particular descriptions in these strikingly candid accounts, and from the systematic

---

[1] James, William. 1987. *Writings, 1902-1910, The Library of America.* New York, N.Y.: Literary Classics of the United States, 3.

juxtaposition of responses written by individuals from a wide variety of faith traditions.

While James develops, out the particulars he assembles, a set of arguments about the nature and significance of religious experience, the aim of Brown's collection is different, not to say more modest. Still, that great predecessor provides a useful point of reference. James's book marked a turning point in the study of religion, incorporating into the historically oriented work of the 19th century a greater concern with, and new theories about, the psychological and "pragmatic" dimensions of religious experience. It is interesting to consider—more than a century later—whether and to what degree these developments in the study of religion by scholars has influenced the self-articulation of individuals who report on their own experiences now.

Brown's collection presents a snapshot of religious experience two decades into the 21st century. Not a comprehensive survey with aspirations to quantitative rigor, it offers rather qualitative data, unvarnished accounts that appear to come from the heart, with minimal interference from the editor. Here we find individuals from different faith traditions speaking in their own ways, using their own language, to describe their experiences. It seems evident—to this reader, at least—that some responses would not have seemed out of place a hundred, some even a thousand or more, years ago, while others betray a 21st century sensibility.

Toward the beginning of his book, James distinguishes between "two orders of inquiry", one which is concerned with the nature, origin, and history of something and results in what he calls an existential judgment, and another which is concerned with the importance, meaning, or significance of the thing, and issues in a value judgment (13). In the present volume, Brown is engaged in both kinds of inquiry, although he is careful not to conflate them. In one question, for example, he asks about the religion's "historical path" and its "evolution," which in James's language would be an existential matter. In another question, he asks, "is it necessary for a person to be an adherent of your religion to be good?," which in essence is asking for a judgment of value. As James points out, such kinds of judgments cannot be deduced immediately from one another. To understand their relation, it is necessary first to separate them analytically, and then to coordinate them. It is one of the virtues of Brown's approach that, through his questioning, he prompts his interviewees to make that first analytical step, and through the presentation, he makes this apparent to the reader.

Although Brown puts the spotlight on his respondents, inevitably an image of the editor emerges from general approach and the specific language and sequencing of the questions. There is a systematic, even scientific, cast of mind at work here. Again, the mode is qualitative, not quantitative, but there is methodological rigor: all the same questions, asked in the same order, and via the same medium. There is, in addition, a manifest commitment to comparative study. One may hazard to guess that a number of the questions posed in this study—e.g., "what is the proper and best role of a human being?"; "what can people do to improve themselves?"—are not merely academic for Brown. In this light, it is noteworthy that his approach is comparatist. Whatever his own doubts or convictions, Brown demonstrates in this project a broad-minded, liberal curiosity. The questions are also informed by a philosophical sensibility, as they address, explicitly and distinctly, matters of ethical, ontological, and metaphysical import. Perhaps most significantly, this is the work of a scholar who is willing to listen. The questions are designed to draw out from his interviewees precisely the kind of "particulars" that, according to James, "make us wiser." Brown then allows these first person accounts to speak for themselves. The result is an illuminating set of reflections and a model for thoughtful inquiry into matters of ultimate significance.

Thomas   Bartscherer,   PhD

Introduction

There are faith leaders in every locale and every generation. They are concerned with the soul and with the pocketbook; they espouse love and according to the news some espouse death; they inspire and they browbeat; and they are as unlike and as like spiritually as the men and women they purport to lead. Some are truly saintly as we would like to think of our saints, some are Rasputins or Richelieus. Some have hearts of gold and feet of clay. They make more and less of scripture and of conscience. And they talk about God.

How are we to think about God? Possibly in the way we think about the world: as rational creatures we can be certain of nothing, but we need no proof of our loves, or of our moments of spiritual connection when we are lucky enough to achieve them.

Does having a faith bring us closer to each other? Although most respondents were people within a religious tradition, what they experience spiritually seems quite different. Are followers of the Abrahamic God closer to each other than to a Sikh? Perhaps not. But these people and others, displaying uniquely human behavior, may participate in religious ritual or prayer, and may perceive behind their physical, spiritual and ethical lives a force, being or creator greater than they are.

Faith doctrines are personal. Respondents were brought into their respective faiths through discussion, friends, clergy, psychedelic experiences and upbringing. Individuals are not founts of doctrine, and ten people who might identify their faith traditions similarly might also have entirely distinct versions of some underlying idea. But behind it all are their ideas of God.

This small book has been a start for me to see in a fashion some similarities and differences among faiths, to bring to light a few truths and to quash a misconception or two, and to learn more about myself, my own tradition and my connection to it. I hope it does that for you.

Peter Brown
Seattle, Washington
December 2018

Table of Contents

1. What is your religious orientation – how do you place or define yourself religiously?

Shia Muslim (Twelver)
Evangelical Christian
Shinto
Baptist
Quaker
Zoroastrian
Jewish
Taoist
Muslim
Anglican
Sikh
Episcopalian / Anglo-Catholic
Pentecostal/Calvinist
Multi-Religious
Christian
Catholic
Buddhist

Bahá'í

Atheist

Anglican

Agnostic

Eliminative Materialist, hard determinist, physicalist, moral naturalist, value pluralist, ignostic. I guess you could say it's a type of ancestor worship, or even animism (in the sense that I don't believe moral significance is limited to humans, or even to living things, not in the sense of philosophical idealism)

I don't have a religion

Open ended, minded

Eastern Orthodox

Spiritual

Undefined

Deist

Pan-Religious (Roman Catholic and Buddhist influences)

Church of Jesus Christ of Latter-day Saints (colloquially, "Mormons" or "LDS")

Non-denominational Universalist

Sikh on paths of Sikhi

Jewish (Traditional/Orthodox)

Jewish (Ultraorthodox / Chabad Lubavitch)

2. How did you personally come to your religion?

Shia Muslim (Twelver): Immense comparative religion over a number of years.

Evangelical Christian: family of origin.

Shinto: Through reading and Japanese culture.

Baptist: I was raised Baptist, left for a long time, and personally decided to return.

Quaker: Raised in a "Bible Reading" family of Methodists

Orthodox Zoroastrian: When I was doing research on ancient Persia I found out about it and did research and talked to a mobed. It's been about 6 years now that I have converted.

Quaker: Went to Quaker school, liked the faith.

Jewish: From my parents and the religious community within which I was raised. Also, from the time I was a very young child, based to some extent on my love of history and tradition, I was taken with Orthodox Judaism. In my fifth grade autobiography, written when

I was 10 or 11 years old, I wrote that I wanted to be an Orthodox Jew when I grew up "because I love my religion." I actually was saying that long before fifth grade, I think.

Taoist when pressed: The Daodejing.

Sunni Muslim (Qadiri Sufi): I was raised into it, but did most of my research on my own.

Anglican: Friends at university.

Sikh: born into family belonging to Sikh faith.

Jewish (Agnostic Secular): Born a secular Jew (which is an ethnicity, culture and religion) in Israel; agnosticism, still reading and thinking.

Episcopalian; Anglo-Catholic: Through joining a choir and searching spiritually on my own, aided by life circumstance.

Pentecostal/Calvinist: Raised in it.

Taoist: Dudeism.

No religion, just the Tao: I don't remember, nor do I wish to.

Multi-Religious: by studying and practicing multiple religions.

Christian: Raised evangelical. Became atheist as a teen. Searched and read in college and young adulthood. Tried an Episcopal church and now attend regularly.

Sunni Muslim: Birth.

Quaker (follower of George Fox): I came to my position by answering the call of God to come out of man-made religion and to enter into revelation, where I know Him by hearing and following His voice.

Anglican: Was raised in it.

Catholic: I'm a convert. It's a long story. I was born in a non-practicing Eastern-Orthodox household. I eventually went into Neo-Pagan stuff and really believed that atheism had it right (at least rationally) but that from an irrational point of view I still believed in a higher power. Eventually guilt over some things I had done took the better of me and combined with research it led me to Catholicism. I didn't want to become Catholic but it seemed genuinely reasonable and I could not disbelieve it, no matter how much I tried. That's the short version at least.

Born Again Christian: The Lord showed me His Grace, the Cross, and my sin. I believed on the Lord Jesus God Jesus Christ for my salvation.

Anglo-Catholic: Boyfriend brought me to church.

Christian: Adult conversion.

Buddhist: I had a powerful experience on a large dose of a psychedelic and after about a year of research trying to understand that experience I settled on Zen Buddhism.

Bahá'í: Grew up in a Baha'i family, decided to declare my faith when I was 15 (age of maturity for Baha'is), and became very active after my pilgrimage to Haifa and Akka when I was 17.

Atheist: Over 15 years of learning about different religions, reading their holy books and learning their rules. It wasn't a light decision.

Christian – Anglican: A mystical experience followed by several weeks of study.

Christian – Anglican: I did a lot of reading on the internet and had experiences to rely on from my childhood.

Agnostic: No one influenced me, I simply came to it over time and realized it made the most sense to me.

Eliminative Materialist: Debate and repeatedly asking "why"?

Chinese Buddhist with Taoist Leanings: Reading and practicing; books on Buddhism and Taoism came first, followed by Eckhart Tolle and Alan Watts lectures. In formal practice, Chan Buddhism has both a local temple and a good fit for my tastes so I go there for formal practice.

I don't have a religion: I don't have one. I gave up on religion for reality.

Taoist: Various English translations of The Tao Te Ching.

Religious Society of Friends (Quaker): It was recommended by a friend who was a member.

Agnostic Buddhist: Exploration. I tried a bunch of religions, got baptized a lot. I was always searching because I feel something but none of them made any sense logically to me. I am a lover of the scientific method. No matter how many churches or religions I tried, I was never completely satisfied. I always felt I couldn't possibly believe any of this, because I have no definitive proof. I then stopped altogether and wondered a bit. I still do not like religions that tell you what to believe based on some guys who said they spoke to "God" or whatever. I fell into Buddhism when my sister started reading about it. I, honestly, lapped it up. Here is a religion that teaches and does not preach. You are, for the most part, responsible for yourself in the end. You are your own judge. I don't know how other people do it, but I can never successfully lie to myself. I do not consider myself a complete Buddhist, which is where the agnostic part comes in. I am not a vegetarian. I do not live in a monastery or as a pilgrim. I love the Buddhist teachings, but unless I am willing to do those things and much more, I do not feel like I can ever truly be a Buddhist. I also believe in something. I do not feel completely alone. I do not think I will cease to exist when I die. Maybe it is for comfort, but I have had too many coincidences throughout my life to believe in absolutely nothing. I also still feel like a scientist in the way that I will never be able to fathom what I cannot perceive or that I have not, or cannot, remember experiencing. I will never truly know until I have come to that point of complete understanding, as I will when I get there. I will try my best to learn as much as I can, to help those I can affect, to try as much as I am able to be a decent human. I am not perfect. I will make mistakes. I will try to learn from those mistakes, but I know I will make some mistakes again. I have accepted this. I have accepted my uncertainty and my shortcomings. I accept that I am not perfect. I'm just going to have fun with what I have and enjoy every little thing that sparks something in me. I will make my own way.

Quaker (Christian): Through many years of agnosticism and personal reflection. I was a rather moody high schooler who saw no good in religion but felt there was a God.

Taoist: Self-study primarily.

Jewish, mainly Reform: By birth. Renewed faith in college.

Daoist: Playing with the I Ching, reading the Dao De Jing.

Daoist: I was initiated into it by an immigrant from China through a martial arts club.

Open ended, minded: I never came to it, it came to me.

Eastern Orthodox: By reading the Bible out of curiosity, then attending a Sunday service (Divine Liturgy) and seeing the content of the Bible fully presented, actualized, and executed in two hours. I was extremely impressed and decided to come back.

Eastern Orthodox: Through months of intellectual and spiritual journey and research.

Spiritual: Raised Catholic, did not agree with the concept growing up.

Eastern Orthodox: Growing distaste for Protestantism, family history.

Daoist: Reading.

Undefined: Personal experience.

Taoist: By practicing qigong for health.

Sunni Muslim: Born into it.

Deist: I was raised Mormon, and that didn't seem very correct, and after the study of several traditional Christian faiths as well as things like Buddhism/Taoism I've come to the conclusion that there is something more. Whether it be the Christian God or a combined nirvana, I am still unsure.

Buddhist with a splash of Christianity, Taoism and Raja Yoga: Realized I was suffering a lot. Secular paths weren't working too well. So I went to a meditation retreat which changed my life fundamentally.

Muslim: Born Muslim.

Buddhist: My interest in Buddhism began with a single conversation with a Buddhist. In that moment a spark was lit and I began studying the Buddhist scripture.

Pan-religious (Roman Catholic and Buddhist influences): I think of it more like religion came to me, as opposed to I came to "it". I was born with a great thirst for spiritual knowledge, and the first 'religion' that came to me was when my mother converted to Catholicism when I was a toddler, and had me baptized as well. I went through a deep personal exploration of a facet of that faith for years. Buddhism and Taoism also found me, and I experienced new facets of the divine through those

Eastern traditions. In the past few years, I've been dancing with animistic magic and fortunetelling traditions. It all coheres to a whole.

Church of Jesus Christ of Latter-Day Saints: I was born into the Church. My parents are both members - my father also born into the Church and my mother a convert. Though raised in the Church, I developed my own faith and testimony through prayer, self-reflection, and scripture study. Throughout my life I experienced many moments that confirmed or reconfirmed my faith.

Non-denominational Universalist: I was born and brought up in a family that already practiced this religion. However, I make consistent efforts to learn and add to my knowledge through constant introspection to connect myself with the Universal Intelligence like the one which subconsciously operates in human beings and other living creatures to regulate our breath, heart, endocrine system, processing of food into vital energy and all cells of the body. This intelligence cannot be explained within the physical limits of our body and mind but is realized and living creatures mingle with it.

Sikh on paths of Sikhi: Family and youth summer camps.

Jewish (Traditional/Orthodox): Raised Jewish, more observant beginning in my twenties.

Jewish (Ultraorthodox / Chabad Lubavitch): As a teenager I attended a class on Chassidic philosophy.

3. What are the most fundamental beliefs of your religion?

Shia Muslim (Twelver): Oneness of God, Prophethood of Muhammad, Infallibility (on Qur'anic interpretation) of the Twelve Imams and that the Qur'an is the word of God.

Evangelical Christian: The Creator is a loving (albeit holy) God who desires a personal relationship with those made in His image. To communicate His nature, God became a human being so we would be able to understand. Jesus Christ is the visible expression of the Creator. He lived a perfect life and died a substitutionary death to meet the holy requirements of the Creator. His defeat of death confirms that the sacrifice offered on the cross was acceptable to the Creator. Jesus is the means by which humanity can be forgiven for their sin and live forever.

Shinto: Kami are everywhere and inhabit everything of natural origin (and some man-made things as well). Be respectful and grateful to the Kami. Practice misogi to cleanse ourselves of pollution (kegare) accumulated in daily life. Respect others, the environment, our family, our ancestors, and ourselves

Baptist: Salvation comes by the grace of God through his son Jesus, which is accepted in faith, and nothing can (a) earn salvation, or (b) cause us to lose salvation.

Quaker: That of God in all. We need only awaken the Buddha within.

Orthodox Zoroastrian: Good thoughts, good words, good deeds

Quaker: Equality. All the rest – Simplicity, Peace, Integrity, and Community – come from that.

Jewish: That there is absolutely one God, who is not physical, who controls the universe, and who is perfect, eternal, and the primary cause of all existence. That God dictated the Torah (Five Books of Moses: Genesis, Exodus, Leviticus, Numbers, and Deuteronomy) 3331 years ago to Moses letter by letter in Hebrew and that the current Torah is exactly the same as the one given to Moses, who is superior to all other prophets (people to whom God directly communicates), whether living before or after Moses. That we may worship only God. That God punishes evil and rewards good. That there will be a Messiah, followed by resurrection of the dead.

Taoist when pressed: Oneness

Sunni Muslim (Qadiri Sufi): Oneness of God, loving the Prophet, doing good unto others, obeying the commands, and seeking forgiveness.

Anglican: The deity, death, and resurrection of Jesus to atone for the sins of His people.

Sikh: Most fundamental belief are nam japna: continuous remembrance of God all the time. Kirat Karna: Earning an honest living. Vand Chakna: Sharing one's earning with others.

Jewish (Agnostic Secular): Agnosticism (we can't know if God exists or not). Judaism according to Rabbi Hillel: do unto others as you would have them do unto you. Aside from that, "Hear O Israel YHWH is our God, YHWH is one" the Qriat Shma, Maimonides' 13 Tenets and Jews as chosen people.

Episcopalian; Anglo-Catholic: God is present and almighty, made up of the three persons of the Trinity, suffered, and died, was resurrected, and therefore by grace is in the process of redeeming the world from sin and bringing forth a new paradigm in which there is no sin.

Pentecostal/Calvinist: Sola Fide! ["By faith alone!"]

Taoist: Taking it easy and letting things come and go.

No religion, just the Tao: Everything is Tao but it's nothing at the same time.

Multi-Religious: All revealed religions come from one or multiple Deity.

Christian: Summarized in the Nicene Creed.

Sunni Muslim: Peace.

Quaker (follower of George Fox): The most fundamental belief is that God, the Creator, is the God who speaks and calls His creation back into covenant with Himself. This, in brief, is the action of the light of Christ within us. When we yield to the reproofs and guidance of that light, we are given strength and power to walk in obedience to what God requires of us.

Anglican: The Apostles' Creed.

Catholic: Monotheism, the Trinity, the Incarnation, the love and goodness of God, the role of the Passion, the fact of the Resurrection, apostolic succession, the role of grace, Baptism, the Real Presence. This would be the list of the fundamentals.

Born Again Christian: Deity of Jesus Christ, saved by faith alone, and the resurrection of Christ.

Anglo-Catholic: Jesus was born of the Virgin Mary, died on the cross, and was brought back to life.

Christian: There is a God who raises the dead and who is love.

Buddhist: In Buddhism as a whole it would be the Four Noble Truths and the Noble Eightfold Path. In Zen there is an emphasis on direct experience – orthopraxy over orthodoxy. We all have Buddha nature, which is beyond time, space, and conceptual thinking.

Bahá'í: Oneness of God, religion, and humanity. Progressive revelation of God's religion through Divine Educators (Moses, Buddha, Jesus, Muhammad, etc. and currently Baha'u'llah). Equality of women and men. Harmony of science and religion. Personal investigation of truth. God is the Creator, is incomprehensible, and also loving. It is possible for humanity to unite globally with Baha'u'llah's teachings. We are on this material world to develop spiritual qualities for our ongoing journey towards God. The soul is wholly spiritual and is reflected in this world through the physical form of our bodies. We are spiritual beings, and our spiritual qualities go with us to the next world while other aspects of personality bound to the physical world remain here.

Atheist: It's simple, we don't believe there is a God. The caveat is that we are open to evidence. Feelings and anecdotes are not evidence.

Christian – Anglican: That Jesus Christ is the Son of God, who died on the cross for the sins of the world and arose from the dead on the third day, which broke the power of death over mankind.

Christian – Anglican: The Nicene and Apostles' Creed.

Agnostic: I cannot disprove nor prove the existence of a God and I am unsure if one even exists but I'm also not totally against the idea.

Eliminative Materialist: Consciousness is an illusion and emotions can never be a source of morality. One should frame one's life around a goal one personally deduces through logic, and the idea that the rejection of value or existence is a logical absurdity.

Chinese Buddhist with Taoist Leanings: Conscious clarity of mind is important above all else, as it creates oneness with life. When a person is at one with life, they are most at peace and most effective as humans.

I don't have a religion: Truth is based on fact.

Taoist: Taoism acknowledges that, although its ideas are conveyed in writing, the writing itself can't capture its essence. While that might seem minor, I believe it's fundamental, because it acknowledges the role of the reader/thinker in its interpretation. When it comes to 'the Answers', no one person has a better shot than anybody else at getting there. Everyone is equal, and everyone tends to be interested in every other person's interpretations. It's beautiful, actually.

Religious Society of Friends (Quaker): Christ is able to be known within each person, in his heavenly role of prophet, priest, king, bishop, and shepherd.

Agnostic Buddhist: All life is sacred and should be respected. I feel it is much more gray when it comes to humans. I do not take what is not mine. I try not to lie, though I am not always good at it and there are also gray areas here. I can always learn something new, and there will always be something new to learn. Whenever I am mad or upset I must pause and find the root cause: this is difficult to do because of pride. I feel like the only one to swallow my pride in most cases and that makes it more difficult to do each time. Harsh reactions are not always my fault, something I try to remember with others. These are my main foci and objectives. Some are harder than others in different circumstances.

Quaker (Christian): Simple living, reconciliation, personal relationship with Jesus, and pacifism.

Taoist: Balance and harmony through embracing paradox.

Jewish, mainly Reform: Monotheism. Ten Commandments. Community practice. Family.

Daoist: All comes from the Dao, an indescribable entity that allows for all things to arise from nothing.

Daoist: Be like water.

Open ended, minded: To use love as a tool for understanding conflict, despair, or hatred.

Eastern Orthodox: We believe in one God, the Father Almighty, Maker of heaven and earth, and of all things visible and invisible; and in one Lord Jesus Christ, the Son of God, the Only-begotten, begotten of the Father before all ages, Light of Light, Very God of Very God, begotten, not made; of one essence with the Father, by Whom all things were made: Who for us men and for our salvation came down from heaven, and was incarnate of the Holy Spirit and the Virgin Mary, and was made man; and was crucified also for us under Pontius Pilate, and suffered and was buried; and the third day He rose again, according to the Scriptures; and ascended into heaven, and sits at the right hand of the Father; and He shall come again with glory to judge the living and the dead, Whose kingdom shall have no end. And we believe in the Holy Spirit, the Lord, and Giver of Life, Who proceeds from the Father, Who with the Father and the Son together is worshipped and glorified, Who spoke by the Prophets; and we believe in one, holy, catholic, and apostolic Church. We acknowledge one

Baptism for the remission of sins. We look for the Resurrection of the dead, and the Life of the age to come. [The Nicene Creed]

Eastern Orthodox: The Nicene Creed. The worship of the Trinity and of the Messiah that has redeemed us.

Spiritual: Peace with animals and nature.

Eastern Orthodox: No Pope, no Filioque, no Sola Scriptura. See Nicene Creed (no "and the son").

Daoist: There are none. It's not a dogma. It's just a road sign.

Undefined: Karmic philosophy. You get what you put in. Don't take things to seriously. Laugh often.

Taoist: The Tao that can be described is not the real Tao.

Sunni Muslim: oneness of God.

Buddhist with a splash of Christianity, Taoism and Raja Yoga: There is Dukkha; there is the cause of Dukkha; there is the end of Dukkha; there is the path to the end of Dukkha. All our actions matter.

Muslim: There is one and only one God (Allah). He has sent Prophets to guide humans. There will be a judgment day.

Buddhist: Buddhism isn't really about belief, at least not in the normal sense. It is about investigating the Buddha's teachings and trying them for yourself.

Pan-religious (Roman Catholic and Buddhist influences): Having a Zen Buddhist orientation means that I do not hold any beliefs. I see all phenomena as constantly changing movement, dialogue, and story-weaving that has in its center Nothingness. So there is nothing to believe in.

Church of Jesus Christ of Latter-Day Saints: We believe in God, the Eternal Father, in his Son, Jesus Christ, and in the Holy Ghost. We believe they are three distinct beings. We believe in living prophets and the same organization that existed in the primitive Church. We believe all men are made in God's image, that we are His literal spirit sons and daughters. As we now are, God once was, as God now is, we may become. We believe in eternal life and resurrection. We believe families can be sealed together forever (no "til death do us part"). We believe God knows us each personally and listens and answers our prayers. We believe in the priesthood – or power of God. We believe the Bible to be the word of God, as far as it is translated correctly; we also Book of Mormon to be the word of God.

Non-denominational Universalist: Passion for attachment with Source of Creation, compassion for others and dispassion towards oneself. Each human being should earn his/her livelihood through honest labor, share all types of your material resources with others and stand firmly against all types of oppression and exploitation even if that should demand the supreme sacrifice of your life.

Sikh on paths of Sikhi: We live in the Grace of a Singular Divine Force which resides within and unifies everything everywhere. From this our way of life springs forth. This generally includes ensuring equity and equality in our community (social justice), seva (selfless service to those in need), and living a truthful life (economically and morally).

Jewish (Traditional/Orthodox): God exists, and has ordained an important role for the Jewish people in communicating His will for humanity. The nature of that role has been defined in the Torah.

Jewish (Ultraorthodox / Chabad Lubavitch): Belief that Hashem [God] continuously created the world. Both the written and oral Torah come from Hashem and are eternal.

4. What is your religion's historical path? How was it begun, who were its greatest exponents, and how has it evolved?

Shia Muslim (Twelver): It started with Muhammad's gradual reception of the Qur'an but has constantly had many ideological splits (like the Sunnis favoring absolute literalism, leading to Wahhabi terrorism), much of its original knowledge is lost on Sunnis rebelling against the Ahl Bayt for their own selfish goals.

Evangelical Christian: It began as an offshoot of Judaism and was redefined by the teachings of a first century rabbi by the name of Jesus and several of his followers.

Shinto: Shinto has no founder but instead developed out of Japanese folk beliefs and native animism. It has been the primary faith in Japan for thousands of years though it was only given a name in the past thousand years or so.

Baptist: The "Baptist" name likely starts in the 1600s, but there were previous groups called "Anabaptists" who existed prior; that said, we believe there have always been churches which practiced our fundamental doctrinal beliefs. We do not consider ourselves Protestant (i.e. products of the Protestant Reformation).

Quaker: Quakers: Jesus 30 AD. George Fox and others in 17th century England.

Orthodox Zoroastrian: It is unknown when exactly Zoroastrianism was born. During the Sassanid period, Zoroastrianism was influenced by Roman Orthodox Christianity (hence the name Orthodox Zoroastrianism).

Quaker: Started in Europe when folk didn't want to suck up to pompous ass-hats for spiritual salvation. God is within, so get out of here with your original sin and Calvinist gloom and doom. We got persecuted because when religion comes from within, you have no state/ hegemonic power over folk. Started off hot in America (Pennsylvania), and was very into abolitionism. I think we ran a lot of the Underground Railroad. Speaking of anti-slavery / racial equality, I think Bayard Rustin is the most OG Quaker in history.

Jewish: Started when "our father" Abraham (born 3831 years ago) recognized for himself that there could only be one God. Abraham, who was tested by God ten times and passed all ten tests, passed belief in and obedience to the one true God to his son Isaac, who passed it to his son Jacob, who passed it to all his 12 sons, the progenitors of the twelve tribes that made up the Jewish people. After the descendants of Jacob's sons were enslaved by ancient Egypt, "our rabbi/teacher" Moses, guided by God, led us to freedom, after which we received the Torah 3331 years ago, including the written Torah (Five Books of Moses--Genesis, Exodus, Leviticus, Numbers, Deuteronomy) and the Oral Torah, which explains the Written Torah. At that point, Jews became bound to observe the entire Torah (613 commandments) and not just the Seven Commandments given to Noah that are binding on others. From Moses, the Torah was taught through the generations and through the establishment of the ancient Jewish kingdom in Israel about 3000 years ago, the building of King Solomon's Temple (the "First Temple" that was destroyed by ancient Babylonia about 2600 years ago), the building of the Second Temple 70 years later (that was destroyed in the Year 70 of the Common Era by Ancient Rome), and the subsequent dispersal of Jews throughout the world. Every generation contains great exponents of Judaism. Some of the more prominent in the last 2000 years include Rashi (1000s), Maimonides (1100s), Yosef Karo (1500s), Vilna Gaon (1700s), Baal Shem Tov (1700s), Chofetz Chaim (1800s to early 1900s), Abraham Isaac Kook (1800s to 1900s), Rav Moshe Feinstein (1900s), and many, many others. After the Second Temple was destroyed, the sacrificial services described in the Written Torah could no longer be performed and were to some extent replaced by prayer. However, traditional Jews believe that in the Messianic era they will resume, along with the Jewish Kingdom in Israel. The traditional

Orthodox community is divided between those who believe that the current State of Israel is a theological first step towards that ultimate redemption and those who do not so believe. Also, around the time of the destruction of the Second Temple, the Oral Torah was to some extent codified in the Talmud, the learning of which became the foundation of Jewish scholarship.

Taoist when pressed: There was a Big Bang, and now we find ourselves here.

Sunni Muslim (Qadiri Sufi): It started with the Prophet Muhammad and I don't think it has necessarily evolved, but now Islam has been a lot more expounded upon with things like philosophies and such regarding topics like Free Will vs Determinism, Accountability, etc. I like Al Ghazali as a scholar a great deal.

Anglican: God has revealed himself at different times and in various ways. He revealed himself to Abraham and promised to bless the nations through his offspring, the Israelites. We believe Jesus was the fulfilment of such promises made to the people of Israel. He is the promised king and also became the sufficient sacrifice to take the punishment for the sins of his people. This is the faith of the early church, however many have tried to redefine it and change it. The Roman Empire adopted Christianity as its official religion, thus birthing the Roman Church. Many additions and subtractions were made to the faith as it moved from its founding and only sufficient definitional documents. In the 14th and 15th centuries Reformation began to break out as the Roman

Church moved further from the faith. Martin Luther kick-started the breakaway from the Roman church in Germany, John Calvin in France, and eventually Thomas Cranmer in England as they sought to return to God's Word as revealed in the Old and New Testaments. Since the Reformation many have sought to return to the ways of the Roman Church or to liberalize the church. Conservative Reformation based Anglicanism still accounts for 70% of the world's Anglicans.

Sikh: Sikhism evolved in the 15th century, and originated in Punjab (Northern India). The first Sikh Guru was Guru Nanak Dev Ji followed by nine Guru Ji. All of them played an instrumental role in the development of the Sikh faith. Eventually all the teachings and sayings of the ten Gurus have been compiled into one Holy book known as the Guru Granth Sahib, which is also known as the "Living Guru."

Jewish (Agnostic Secular): Judaism evolved naturally and progressively from Canaanite polytheism and monolatric worship of a national God in the Iron Age kingdom of Judah in the first temple following its destruction and the exile to Babylon. The Jews became decentralized and dispersed following the destruction of the second temple of Jerusalem by Romans. Reform and Conservative Judaism, who attempt to be Judaism adapted to modern liberal values, split [from traditional, now called "Orthodox" Judaism] in the 19th century.

Episcopalian; Anglo-Catholic: It branched off from the Roman Catholic (Western) church in England following the Reformation, most notably by Henry VIII due to personal and political disagreements with the Pope. It was furthered by the Reform ideas of Thomas Cranmer and Elizabeth I, and continues to evolve as a worldwide organization of churches.

Pentecostal/Calvinist: I believe Pentecostalism started through revival moments of the early 20th century.

Taoist: Taoism started in ancient China although it didn't really become big until the Renaissance where enlightenment boomed.

No religion, just the Tao: First, Taoism is not a religion. It doesn't have a dogma, but is influenced by sects that originated in China, so it is somewhat mixed with Chinese culture. It began approximately 2,000 years ago. It is said that someone named Lao Zi [also, "Lao Tzu"] wrote a book for someone, the "Tao Te Ching," and from that book people found the Tao.

Multi-Religious: N/A – my religion is eclectic.

Christian: Christianity has its roots in Hellenized Judaism. After Christ, early Christians wrote letters and recorded practices some of which were collected as the Bible, the book of the church. With Constantine it became a proper institution and with the advent of the Reformation multiple denominations were formed.

Sunni Muslim: Prophet Muhammad saw.

Quaker (follower of George Fox): I am surrounded by a "cloud of witnesses" as the writer of the book of Hebrews put it. Abraham is called the father of faith and our faith is called the faith of Abraham because we, like him, must hear the voice of the living God calling us out of cultural religion and must go where God's voice leads us. One might say George Fox began the Quaker movement, yet he is but one of many who have responded to God's call to follow His voice. We, who have turned from our own ways to walk in His way, are following the One who is eternal, in whom there are no shifting shadows, who is the same yesterday, today, and forever. Faithfulness today may require things different from faithfulness yesterday because circumstances today are different than yesterday, but all who witness this covenant with God can testify to the unity that only comes from following His voice. There is no evolution, no change, in the requirements of righteousness. The changes that have come within Christendom since the days of the Apostles are the result of not listening to the voice of God.

Anglican: Christ founded Christianity, but it has splintered and quarreled over questions of Reform.

Catholic: It began with Jesus Christ. As for exponents .... well, there are the twelve Apostles and other early figures like Irenaeus and Augustine, others like Aquinas, Catherine of Sienna and Francis of Assisi, and more modern examples like John Paul II.

Born Again Christian: Started with Christ, and through the Anabaptists.

Anglo-Catholic: King Henry VIII and Elizabeth I.

Christian: Judaism, Jesus, the apostles, the church, schism, Reformation, revival.

Buddhist: Bodhidharma brought his version of Buddhism to China, where it interacted with Chinese Taoism and developed into Chan Buddhism. Zen is the Japanese version of the word "Chan." The early exponents were the first patriarchs: Huike, Huineng, Mazu etc. The Japanese version of Zen seems much more formalized and overly serious compared to those early patriarchs.

Bahá'í: We believe in one religion, so view God's message to us as having begun through His first Manifestation. More recently, and officially/specifically in the history of the Baha'i Faith, it began in 1844. In the midst of millennialism in Christianity and Islam, the Bab ("Gate" in Arabic/Farsi) claimed to be the Promised One of Islam and the Herald of the Promised One of all religions (return of Christ, etc.). The Babi Faith faces much persecution from the Muslim clergy and Persian/Ottoman governments. The teachings of the Bab were groundbreaking in many ways but were primarily purposed to change Islam (viewed widely as unchangeable for all time) and prepare humanity for the coming of the Promised One (referred to as Him Whom God Shall Make Manifest in the Writings of the Bab). The religion grew fast and among the prominent followers was Mirza Husayn Ali, although he never met the Bab. After the Bab was martyred and executed by the government, Baha'u'llah was imprisoned and claimed there to receive His first revelation that He was the

Promised One (1852). In 1863 He publicly announced His mission. For decades He was banished by the Persian and Ottoman governments in efforts to extinguish His Faith. This simply caused it to grow. He revealed a large amount of writings as guidance from God for humanity today. His message focused on uniting humanity. He revealed spiritual, mystical, and legal teachings. He appointed His eldest son Abdul-Bahá as the authorized interpreter of His Writings after His passing, and as the center of His Covenant that all Baha'is are to turn. His interpretations and expounding are authoritative, and are valuable to Baha'is to this day. He traveled through Europe and to North America spreading the Faith and offering guidance to Baha'i communities. He appointed His grandson as interpreter after Him (Shoghi Effendi). Shoghi Effendi expanded the Faith and its administration greatly in his lifetime. He left no children and did not appoint an interpreter in his stead. Baha'u'llah designed a democratically elected institution called the House of Justice, to administer in each city, country, and one for the planet. It was elected several years after Shoghi Effendi's passing, with near universal participation of all countries. Since then, the administrative order has grown greatly and has become more complex. Baha'i scholarship has increased greatly although much work is needed. Scriptures have been translated further and published. The Faith has grown greatly in number to over 5 million (registered to vote in Baha'i elections). Most importantly, the teaching work of Baha'is has grown organically into community building activities where Baha'is and their friends learn how to apply and spread Baha'u'llah's teachings to solve humanities problems. Those involved are in ever greater number not registered Baha'is, but Baha'is at heart or just friends of the Faith. The activities include Spiritual classes for children that include lessons on prayer, spiritual qualities, and the history of the world's religions; junior youth groups where Baha'i teachings are explored in service to the community in a completely non-religious way (this is where large participation of non-registered Baha'is participate); and devotional gatherings where the members of the community come together and pray and share in elevated conversation in an effort to build bridges and form unity. All of these efforts have grown greatly over a series of global plans and initiatives. The bicentenary of Baha'u'llah's birth just passed and that of the Bab is about to occur, marking periods of increased activity and celebration.

Atheist: My dad's family was Southern Baptist and my mom tried but didn't succeed. I went to church off and on as a kid, often getting kicked out for asking too many questions. I was just trying to understand but it was seen as disrespect. As a teenager I realized Christianity wasn't for me. I liked Christ alright and live a lot like he taught, but I'm not judgmental and won't stop speaking to a person because their beliefs are different from mine. As a young adult I studied the other Abrahamic religions and found that they are all extremely similar. Went to eastern religions like Hindu, Taoism, Buddhism and again these rules made no sense to me. I have always been a woman of science and like to learn about things, but I need concrete evidence to believe in something. So I took the best parts of all religions and live my life being the best person I can be.

Christian – Anglican: It began with Jesus and the Apostles in the 1st Century AD and later Reformed in both the 16th century AD by the English Reformers and again in the 19th century by the Tractarians. It began as Catholicism, then became very Protestant before settling down into the *via media* between the two groups.

Christian – Anglican: Jesus Christ, the Apostle Paul, and countless others. It has evolved from small communities to one of the most powerful ideas in the world.

Agnostic: Apparently the term was coined in 1869 but considering it's mostly lack of faith then this question doesn't apply a whole lot.

Eliminative Materialist: In New England almost 20 years ago, just a group of high school kids (for full disclosure, I was among them), debated among themselves on the nature of the meaning of life. It went through a quick wave. Many people interested in the project gradually moved away, lost interest, or married into other religions, and it's just starting to go into its second generation now.

Chinese Buddhist with Taoist Leanings: Raised Catholic (thus I am not Catholic).

I don't have a religion: Atheism attracts many popular people like Carl Sagan, AronRa, Thomas Westford and Richard Dawkins.

Taoist: Laozi wrote a book over a millennium ago, one that really tapped into something unique. People have been enjoying it since!

Religious Society of Friends (Quaker): It began in mid-17th century England when its first proponent, George Fox, inwardly "heard a voice which said, 'There is one, even Christ Jesus that can speak to thy condition.' When [he] heard it, [his] heart did leap for joy. Then the Lord let me see why there was none upon the earth that could speak to [his] condition, namely that [he] might give him all the glory. For all are concluded under sin, and shut up in unbelief, as [he] had been, that Jesus Christ might have pre-eminence, who enlightens, and gives grace, faith, and power" (Works of George Fox, vol. 1, p. 74). George Fox then traveled throughout England, and his preaching gathered many adherents who were likewise empowered to preach the Word of God (Christ), and Friends meetings, i.e. gatherings, were formed. Three hundred and seventy years have passed, and today there are several branches of Quakerism: Liberal, Evangelical, and Conservative. Liberals do not recognize Christ as the center of their meetings; Evangelicals are not different from Protestants, and Conservatives largely retain the original faith.

Agnostic Buddhist: I am not sure how to answer this. I have found my own path through other ideas (if we are talking Buddhism). It has been based on a teacher through time. One that, through many lives, has found a way to be what is best in human qualities. Buddhism has evolved around the concept of compassion being the ultimate achievement: to give of yourself for others even at a cost to yourself if necessary. Buddha, or a bodhisattva, are the main components to strive to imitate, Buddha's being the path to follow, and a bodhisattva being a goal to achieve – a teacher who sacrificed anything and everything to ensure enlightenment in others. There are many types of Buddhism. I am unsure from which ones I have picked. I strive for compassion and understanding.

Quaker (Christian): The Religious Society of Friends, better known as Quakers, began in the middle to late 1600s. It came about as one of many Reform movements within the Anglican Church. In stark contrast to the Puritans of the time, Quakers began as a much more open group willing to accommodate all peoples. In fact, there were female ministers as early as the 1640s. By the 1780s Quakers were establishing themselves as progressives and most notably Abolitionists. The man credited with founding the movement is George Fox and the best known American Quaker was William Penn, the founder of Pennsylvania. Over the years Quakers have evolved from creating the modern prison system and solitary confinement to being some of the staunchest opponents of it today. It has seen many splits over time but remains an overall progressive and inclusive group despite being almost entirely white.

Taoist: [This demands a] long answer! Start with proto-Taoism c. 1600 BCE, through contemporary Taoist and Taoist adjacent teachers and exemplars.

Jewish, mainly Reform: Ancient, formed when man rose from polytheism. Most fiercely observed in the time of the Temple but modernized after its sacking (twice over).

Daoist: A mixture of academic philosophy and local religions, with many different currents in the modern day.

Daoist: It is a philosophy that started with the 5 pecks of rice group in the Yellow Turban Rebellion at the end of the Han Dynasty in China.

Open ended, minded: Who can know such things for certain? All that was is now faded memory. It matters not.

Eastern Orthodox: The Orthodox Catholic Church, also called the Eastern Orthodox Church, was founded in the 1st Century AD by Jesus of Nazareth, the Messiah or Christ, and immediately administered by His twelve disciples after His Ascension. The doctrines transmitted by Jesus and kept by the apostles are taught by the bishops, who have a line of succession coming from the apostles themselves. Seven Church-wide councils were held in its history to condemn certain heresies and define better the faith. The first two councils (Nicaea I and Constantinople I) address the divinity of Jesus and the divinity of the Holy Spirit; the third, fourth, fifth, sixth, and seventh councils address the reality of the

Incarnation (the relationship between Jesus's humanity and Jesus's divinity). The first council was held in 325 and the seventh was held in 787. There is not a single saint who is recognized as embodying the fullness of Orthodox teaching and tradition, but there are certain groups of saints that have special status. Notably among them are the Three Holy Hierarchs, who are recognized as being excellent exponents of the faith: St. John Chrysostom; St. Basil the Great; and St. Gregory of Nazianzus. Several heretical sects have broken away from the Church, notably the Church of the East in the 5th century, the Oriental Orthodox Church in the 5th century, the Catholic Church in the 13th century, and the True Orthodox Church in the 20th Century. Today the Eastern Orthodox Church consists of 15 autocephalous (self-governing and administratively independent) churches: Constantinople, Alexandria, Antioch, Jerusalem, Russia, Serbia, Bulgaria, Romania, Georgia, Greece, Cyprus, Albania, Czech lands and Slovakia, Poland, and America.

Eastern Orthodox: Started in ~33 AD, and not much has changed since. We have made decisions defining certain dogmas, as for example canonization of the Bible in the 5th Century.

Spiritual: Catholic. I disowned them for their abuse of children.

Eastern Orthodox: See Nicene Creed. Started in 1st Century.

Daoist: I was raised Methodist if that's what you're asking. They couldn't answer my questions to my satisfaction.

Undefined: It all started when I was born. I was definitely its greatest exponent. It has evolved to the tender age of 23.

Taoist: I believe that it originates in prehistory. It appears to have roots in animism.

Sunni Muslim: Islam started in the Middle East. Much of Africa and Asia is Muslim today.

Buddhist with a splash of Christianity, Taoism and Raja Yoga: The story goes that the Siddhartha Gotama discovered this path and began teaching it to others some 2,500 years ago. I don't think that story matters much, though. It was not written down or even written about until at least 100 years after his death. It has changed throughout history drastically; Buddhism changes in every country goes to.

Muslim: It began when the first human, Adam, was given a soul. Then he was addressed by Allah directly. Then as humanity evolved and times changed, Allah sent various Prophets towards humans. The last of them was Prophet Muhammad PBUH ["peace be upon him" – 'alayhi s-salām' or (عليه السلام)]. There is only one religion of God and currently it is present in the form of Quran.

Buddhist: Siddhartha Gotama, the son of the king of the Sakyan tribe, went forth on his noble search to find a way to bring suffering to an end. In its basic sense Buddhism really hasn't evolved all that much over the past 2,500 years. There are different traditions/sects/schools that all have a lineage going back to the first Buddhist community.

Pan-religious (Roman Catholic and Buddhist influences): Given that I am awake to metaphysical dimensions of reality rather than a following a "religion", I will say that most humans in history have experienced what I experience: a sense of awe and creative, constantly evolving interaction with That Which is Greater.

Church of Jesus Christ of Latter-Day Saints: The modern Church was founded by God through the boy-prophet Joseph Smith in the 19th Century in the ·northeastern United States. However, we believe that the Church is the same as the ancient Church from the Bible, and that it has been restored through the prophet to the Latter-days after plain and precious truths were lost following the deaths of Christ and the apostles. The priesthood keys to lead the Church and receive revelation for the whole earth were lost as the prophets and apostles were all killed. Now, that authority is restored to the earth again through the Prophet Russell M. Nelson.

Non-denominational Universalist: It began with Sri Guru Nanak Dev Ji [born 1469] who brought out the futility of illogical rituals prevalent in the then prevailing religions, particularly the Hindu religion, and showed people the right path through discussions/interaction with religious heads of other faiths, be these Hindus, Muslims, Yogis and others claiming to have some supernatural powers. All his writings and those of other Sikh Gurus and a large number of various devotees hailing from different religions, sects and beliefs were compiled by the 5th Guru Sri Guru Arjun Dev Ji in what Sikhs worship as their living Guru – Sri Guru Granth Sahib. It is pertinent to state that after considering all religious writings, the United Nations declared Sri Guru Granth Sahib as the supreme written version about religion.

Sikh on paths of Sikhi: It arose out of an era of gross societal inequality in order to empower any person to attain spiritual freedom. Started after the 1st Nanak (Guru Nanak Sahib) had a revelation and became a prophet in the late 15th Century. He wrote Divine-inspired scriptures and travelled the world, spreading his message through song and leading by example. He passed leadership on through nine more successors who continued the revolution of equality through spiritual, mental, physical, economic, and social trajectories. The 10th Nanak (Guru Gobind Singh Sahib) formalized the leadership of Sikhi into two aspects: 1) Guru Granth Sahib – the spiritual leader, a compilation of the Divine-inspired scriptures written by the Sikh Gurus as well as other spiritual leaders with similar views; and 2) Guru Khalsa Pantha – a community of committed Sikhs who would forge ahead as active participants and doers of the revolution of Love and Equality as guided by Guru Granth Sahib. Over time the Guru Khalsa Panth has manifested in different ways depending on the era. But the spiritual core that all Sikhs unanimously agree on still and forever will reside in the Divine-inspired words of the Guru Granth Sahib.

Jewish (Traditional/Orthodox): God's existence was revealed to Abraham; 10 generations later, Moses and the people of Israel received the Torah. Since much of that information was transmitted in an oral tradition from generation to generation, we've been arguing about it ever since. The most significant of those arguments were transmitted in the Talmudic period (First Century through Sixth Century of the Common Era).

Jewish (Ultraorthodox / Chabad Lubavitch): It began at Sinai and great religious leaders in every generation assured its continuity. It is the same and has not evolved.

Peter Brown

5. What sort of clergy does your religion have, and what roles do they play?

Shia Muslim (Twelver): None, only authority from Muhammad, Fatimah and Twelve Imams (which lies in scripture and historical records).

Evangelical Christian: Our clergy consists of pastors (male and female) who are called by individual congregations. In addition to planning and leading weekly worship services, they teach and explain the Scriptures. They perform the sacred rites of baptism and holy communion.

Shinto: Mainly priests, who care for the Kami, perform rituals and blessings and Miko, who prepare offerings, dance for the Kami and help out around the shrine.

Baptist: Pastors offer leadership and guidance to the congregation, and preach sermons based on the texts of the Bible.

Quaker: No clergy.

Orthodox Zoroastrian: Mobeds are the Zoroastrians priests that arrange the ceremonies or help one that seeks help, whether religious or not.

Quaker: No clergy.

Jewish: They are called rabbis and are theologically not considered to have any special powers different from other Jews, thus differing from the role that priests play in the Catholic Church, for instance. Rabbis are seen as learned and wise scholars of Jewish Law and tradition whose major roles are to teach that Law and tradition and to decide, based on their knowledge, questions of Jewish Law. Traditional Judaism does maintain that when our Temple is rebuilt and sacrifices resume, they must be conducted by "Kohanim" or priests, determined strictly by lineage (male line back to Aaron, the brother of Moses). That lineage is maintained by traditional Jews to this day.

Taoist when pressed: None.

Sunni Muslim (Qadiri Sufi): There is no real Clergy, just the Imam that leads the prayer

Anglican: Each congregation had at least one pastor teacher. The role is to teach new people from the word of God and to lead and correct them.

Sikh: There is no ordained priesthood in Sikhism. Learned, knowledgeable practicing Sikhs known as Gyani or Granthis lead the prayers and reads the Guru Granth Sahib to the worshippers at Sikh temples known as Gurudwaras.

Jewish (Agnostic Secular): Rabbis which are more or less respected authorities on Judaism and community leaders. Can't really say more than that; I am not religious and go to a synagogue maybe once a year.

Episcopalian; Anglo-Catholic: There is a threefold clergy, consisting of bishops, priests, and deacons, although many deacons are "transitional" on the way to priesthood. Typically a congregation is led by a priest (rector or vicar in most cases), but sometimes by a deacon. Clergy celebrate the Eucharist and lead in spiritual formation for the congregation in order to empower the laity to take on part of the governance and maintenance of the church.

Pentecostal/Calvinist: Pastors: they teach scripture and organize the church.

Taoist: Dudeist priest, abiding.

No religion, just the Tao: It's a sectarian "religion;" there are different temples and things like that for every belief, but in the basic Taoism pursuit there are no clergy.

Multi-Religious: N/A

Christian: Depends on denomination. Pastors/priests are like teachers, counselors, and administrators for a nonprofit; they ideally hold the orthodox line.

Quaker (follower of George Fox): We have no clergy because we gather to know Christ Jesus, the Word which was in the beginning, present in our midst in all His offices. Whether or not there are spoken words, we wait to hear Christ and to know His functions in and among us as His people.

Anglican: It has three orders: deacons, priests, bishops. They administer its rites, consecrate one another, govern the Church, and oversee parish life.

Catholic: There is an organized clergy, as everybody knows. Priests administer the sacraments and in theory should try to be good leaders of their flock (though sadly this does not always happen). Besides these pastoral functions and administering sacraments bishops have a teaching authority and so does the Pope.

Born Again Christian: Pastors and deacons as 1 Timothy 3 explains.

Anglo-Catholic: Priests and bishops.

Christian: Pastor and deacon.

Buddhist: There are rishis – masters who oversee a monastery. In America, many rishis and monks are not full time and lead lay lives outside of the monastery.

Bahá'í: No clergy. Elected bodies of 9 individuals that administer and legislate law. Other roles exist but none with interpretative or legislative authority. Elected bodies cannot interpret either, except when implicit in the application of law.

Atheist: Technically there are different types of atheists such as the church of Satan and the church of the flying spaghetti monster. These are really just responses to the notion that without a God we are amoral. We don't officially have any sort of clergy.

Christian – Anglican: Anglicanism (and my church – the Episcopal Church – specifically) have an episcopal structure of bishop > priest > deacon. The clergy come from an unbroken line from the Apostles and, as such, are the ones ordained to bless the sacrament and lead the people of the Church.

Christian – Anglican: They confect the Eucharist.

Agnostic: None

Eliminative Materialist: We're not a large enough religion to have a dedicated class of clergy, and we're quite anti-hierarchy so there are no roles that are really exclusive to anyone. The biggest thing is that to oversee other people doing ritual debating or to oversee someone's rite of passage you have to have already had your own rite of passage.

Chinese Buddhist with Taoist Leanings: Monastic group in the formal temple I attend, led by an abbess and with a few female monks. Below them are lay volunteers and practitioners.

I don't have a religion: There is no clergy.

Taoist: My answer should be more nuanced, because there are regional differences, but in general none. Every Taoist interprets directly, and encourages others to do the same.

Religious Society of Friends (Quaker): In our original faith, Christ was to guide each person and the community as a whole in worship and decisions necessary for all areas of life. As Quaker faith has changed over the centuries, each branch has dealt differently with matters of worship and practice. Among Liberals, humanistic ideals and values are guides; among Evangelicals, Protestant faith and practice prevail; among Conservative, the smallest group, the inward Christ remains central to worship and group practices.

Agnostic Buddhist: In Buddhism, at least the times I have had an opportunity to attend, have been with a central teacher of sorts who demonstrates and teaches different aspects of how to recognize your own compassion. Then how to implement it more often and more naturally. As to myself, I do not attend anything. I do not have clergy. I live by example to those around me if I am able.

Quaker (Christian): We have ministers who serve as guides. I belong to Liberal Quakerism which incorporates some elements of traditional Protestantism. In my community our minister teaches lessons from the Bible and leads us in thanksgiving.

Taoist: Monks, priests, nuns, hermits … There are many "clergy" within the many sects of Taoism.

Jewish, mainly Reform: Rabbis are our community and spiritual leaders.

Daoist: The clergy mainly practice rites for the benefit of their own spiritual development, but also perform communal rites for the lay community.

Daoist: We have "Daoshis," who aren't like Western clergy. They are more like shamans or wizards.

Open ended, minded: None. Clergies maintain the status quo. Mostly old men and women too afraid of death or change to help anyone spiritually.

Eastern Orthodox: There are three major orders: the bishops, the priests (or presbyters), and the deacons. The bishops are the successor of the apostles, appointed by God to guard the Orthodox tradition and teach it to their flock. Because the bishop cannot be everywhere at the same time, he appoints priests who function as the spiritual fathers of the local community, being given the authority by the bishop to administer sacraments and to teach the faithful. The deacons work to help the priest during the Divine Liturgy, serve the community, and administer the Eucharist (communion).

Eastern Orthodox: Deacons serve the priests liturgically. Priests shepherd their parishes. Bishops shepherd their dioceses. Archbishops/Patriarch shepherd their archdioceses/churches.

Spiritual: None.

Eastern Orthodox: Priests, Bishops. Tend to services and to laity.

Daoist: We just talk.

Undefined: A man in a punk rock band tee. Leading by example.

Taoist: I don't really know. There are none around where I live.

Sunni Muslim: Imams, spiritual purposes.

Buddhist with a splash of Christianity, Taoism and Raja Yoga: Monks, I suppose. I am not sure that is a great definition for monks though. They are practicing hard to reduce their suffering. The institution doesn't require that they do anything for others but they do out of compassion for us.

Muslim: A group from within Muslims, who must dedicate their lives to studying Islam and then warn people about the hereafter.

Buddhist: Monks and nuns. Among them there are novices and elders. Buddhism doesn't have a singular governing body. The ordained preserve and transmit the teachings.

Pan-religious (Roman Catholic and Buddhist influences): None

Church of Jesus Christ of Latter-Day Saints: The highest office of the Church is the prophet. We also have the Quorum of the Twelve Apostles, the two Quorums of the Seventy which are regionally assigned. Under the Seventy are the Stake Presidents who supervise around 4-5 individual congregations, which we call wards. At the ward level, the head of the ward is Bishop with two counselors. All the "clergy" in the Church are lay-clergy. The Bishop oversees the welfare of the ward in both spiritual and physical needs. Individual members of the Church are called to leadership positions at various levels, and aside from the Prophet and Apostles, serve in those callings for a limited period of time, typically from three to five years.

Non-denominational Universalist: Unlike Church, we do not have a Clergy. Instead we call this person Preacher – Granthee, who interprets teachings of Guru Granth Sahib and propagates its message to the masses. Besides this, he/she also inspires and provides spiritual direction for uplifting of human beings towards the Source of Creation.

Sikh on paths of Sikhi: Officially there are no clergy, as that would negate the notion of equality and that every person has equal access to the Divine. Nevertheless, in our Gurudwaras (Sikh place of worship), services are conducted by religious scholars known as Granthis or Gyanis, and Kirtan (hymns) are sung by folks called Ragis. Services include recitation of the different Shabads (hymns) of Guru Granth Sahib. They are spoken, sung, as well as explored and discussed within a service.

Jewish (Traditional/Orthodox): Rabbis lead autonomous communities around the world and come together as possible to explicate and apply the tradition.

Jewish (Ultraorthodox / Chabad Lubavitch): Rabbis who teach and answer question about beliefs and practices.

Peter Brown

6. What are the most important questions a religion can address?

Shia Muslim (Twelver): I think this question can get a bit trivial because a true religion's purpose (functionally) is to provide you with tools to connect WITH the divine - whether Muslim or Hindu.

Evangelical Christian: Who is God? How can God be known? What does God expect of His creation? What hope do humans have of life beyond death? How is eternal life realized?

Shinto: How we can be grateful and happy with our time on Earth.

Baptist: Why are we here, what are we for, and what hope do we have?

Quaker: Find that of God within ourselves and others.

Orthodox Zoroastrian: How should humans behave with each other?

Quaker: How to leave the world better than you found it.

Jewish: The purpose of our existence. What we should accomplish during our time on earth. How we got here in the first place (our origins, both as individuals and as a group). Where we are going (our destiny, both as individuals and as a group).

Taoist when pressed: None.

Sunni Muslim (Qadiri Sufi): the afterlife.

Anglican: The meaning of life. The hope we have for the future. Why the world is the way it is.

Sikh: Depending on what is asked. However many formed religions try to address issues of our mere existence, purpose on this earth, karma, good, bad and evil. The list goes on and on.

Jewish (Agnostic Secular): Is there a supernatural influence on the world? Is there anything supernatural? What happens after death? What is the purpose of life? How should you live a good life?

Episcopalian; Anglo-Catholic: What is my place in the world? How can I be the best version of myself? What is the nature of life, death, and human experience? How can I "make a difference" in the world?

Pentecostal/Calvinist: Morality.

Taoist: How to obtain self-lasting peace.

No religion, just the Tao: No questions, no answers – just the Tao.

Multi-Religious: All questions are equally important but ultimately all questions are unimportant.

Christian: What is it to live a good and moral life; why does this matter; what is the nature of humanity; why do we suffer and die?

Sunni Muslim: Fatwas. [*Editor's note: online definitions of fatwa include "a ruling on a point of Islamic law given by a recognized authority" and "an Islamic religious ruling, a scholarly opinion on a matter of Islamic law."*]

Quaker (follower of George Fox): The most important question that man can ask is how can I/we be remade into the image of God, filled with His life and light?

Anglican: What is the Divine?

Catholic: What's the meaning of life? How can we be happy? Who made us? Why and how did we get here? Is there anybody out there who loves us? What is love? How can we become better people?

Born Again Christian: Salvation, and [living] the rest of your life by the guidance of the Spirit of God.

Anglo-Catholic: Why? Science can answer how, religion can answer why.

Christian: Way of life

Buddhist: Why are we here? What is the point of existence, if any? What is this place all about?

Bahá'í: The problems currently afflicting humanity. Most fundamentally these are the unity of the human race and its spiritual development. To guide an ever advancing civilization. To free humanity from materialism and provide the education necessary for us to thrive. Religion also addresses generally why we are here, who we are, and what we are supposed to do while we are here.

Atheist: Honestly, they are a great source of comfort for people scared of death or the unknown. However, I feel that throughout history organized religion has done far more harm than good.

Christian – Anglican: What is the meaning of life, what happens after death, how can I find fulfillment in my life?

Christian – Anglican: What is the meaning of life?

Agnostic: What can we do while we're here?

Eliminative Materialist: What is good?

Chinese Buddhist with Taoist Leanings: Search for meaning in an increasingly chaotic world, peace, and value systems that are inherently humanistic (as opposed to the view that deities say it so you better do it).

I don't have a religion: Religions only make excuses for the unknown or, in the case of Satanism, push for equality for those lacking gullibility in the supernatural.

Taoist: Anecdotally, I find religions are a way for people to join together to solve problems through role-playing. The idea is often to defer to an out-of-reach all-seeing authority (e.g. Gods) so that people feel freer to share their vulnerabilities, since their deeds are supposedly laid bare regardless; this helps people be vulnerable together and grow together, and motivates them to spread word of the religion.

Religious Society of Friends (Quaker): The most important questions a religion can address is what constitutes right relationship to God for me as a person, and for us as a community? And, what is right relationship with others for me as a person and for ourselves as a community?

Agnostic Buddhist: There are not any, in my opinion. I suppose if someone is unsure of how to be a good, decent person they can seek religion to better themselves. Religion to me is something beyond myself to strive for. I have a pretty good base moral compass, I feel. I use religion to strive for the areas I am weakest in. Such as impatience and anger. I focus on the parts that push me in those areas. But as for the questions that we all have? Like where we come from or where we go in the end or why are we here ... I don't think any religion can completely answer any of those. No matter how compassionate I become through my endeavors I will still not definitively know the answers. Religion should be used as a baseline of how to better yourself in the eyes of acceptance and understanding. Religion is not a cure-all.

Quaker (Christian): How you can be a better person to your neighbor and to all of God's creation.

Taoist: Each religion has a different assessment of the "problem" of the human condition (i.e. Buddhism and Suffering, Christianity and Sin, Islam and Pride). Taoism does not look for a "problem" but a discord that one may experience. The practices and exercises of Taoism are oriented towards bringing one into greater harmony, like tuning an instrument.

Jewish, mainly Reform: Purpose.

Daoist: The purpose of life, how to live, the nature of the self, the world, and the relation between the two.

Daoist: How to become a wise person.

Open ended, minded: How to live well.

Eastern Orthodox: The nature of the created world, the nature of mankind (anthropology) and mankind's relationship with the creation that surrounds him, and why things are and how they should be based on what God has revealed to us.

Eastern Orthodox: How to fulfill one's purpose and role in creation.

Spiritual: Equality above all else. Every living thing deserves to live.

Eastern Orthodox: Why are we here? What do we need to do while we are here?

Daoist: How do I follow the path without getting stuck in a rut? How can I leave the path without getting lost?

Undefined: I think the most important questions a religion can answer are the unspoken ones. Leading by example and helping others discover their own path is the best thing an established religion can do.

Taoist: I don't know.

Sunni Muslim: Morality.

Buddhist with a splash of Christianity, Taoism and Raja Yoga: What are the causes of your current state of being? What actions can you take to produce states of being that are better? What qualities of mind should one develop? How should these qualities be developed?

Muslim: Who is the creator of this Earth, and the universe, and everything that exists inside this universe. Why did He create humans? Why is so much power given to humans? Are we accountable for our powers? What will be the conclusion of this worldly life? What is the value of good actions? Will criminals ever get punishment for their crimes, as in this world only a handful are prosecuted?

Buddhist: The cause of suffering and a way that can end it.

Pan-religious (Roman Catholic and Buddhist influences): What do all phenomena point to? And the answer is nothingness.

Church of Jesus Christ of Latter-Day Saints: Who am I? What is my purpose in this life? Where did I come from? What is truth?

Non-denominational Universalist: Religion needs to address the causes of mankind's sorrow, sufferings and worries emanating from all walks of human life, including the self-created ones, and provide a clearing understanding on how all our ills stem from human greed, anger, lust, materialistic attachments and arrogant attitudes so that all nations and people of each can live together in peace and harmony with others.

Sikh on paths of Sikhi: Whatever questions are important to any person at that moment in time, I suppose. But maybe also the question of what is the meaning of life and how can I grow as a person?

Jewish (Traditional/Orthodox): What does God expect of us and how can he help us achieve happy lives and a better world.

Jewish (Ultraorthodox / Chabad Lubavitch): Man's purpose in life. How to deal with life's challenges.

7. What is the proper and best role of a human being in this world?

Shia Muslim (Twelver): To be in union with the divine will, to have integrity, honesty and true heart.

Evangelical Christian: One who models himself after Jesus. A humble leader who leads by serving. A person of honesty and integrity that loves God and loves others as he loves himself.

Shinto: To love themselves and others, to do their utmost to help everyone they can.

Baptist: To serve others as Christ served us.

Quaker: Finding that of God within and within others.

Orthodox Zoroastrian: Make life pleasant for themselves and others.

Quaker: In service to others.

Jewish: To fear, love, obey and serve God and to try to understand and emulate Him, to the limited extent that we are capable.

Taoist when pressed: Alongside other humans, treating each other and the planet as best we can.

Sunni Muslim (Qadiri Sufi): To obey God, because God is the one who knows best and by obeying Him you are doing the best deed unto others as well as yourself.

Anglican: To love God and enjoy him forever.

Sikh: The proper role is to keep God foremost and be kind, honest, help others and the less fortunate. The best role of a human being is to keep their integrity, be transparent, attuned to others and their own needs. A sense of attunement to themselves and surroundings. Act and react from a place of abundance instead of scarcity and not to be afraid to ask for help when needed.

Jewish (Agnostic Secular): To do unto others.

Episcopalian; Anglo-Catholic: I don't think I can give a complete answer, but I would hope to be kind, just, and humble. It is to look after those with less means than oneself and hold accountable those with power.

Pentecostal/Calvinist: To be a good person and spread God's word.

Taoist: Who knows?

No religion, just the Tao: Be the world.

Multi-Religious: To serve.

Christian: Solidarity with others; service to God and fellow humans; creation and building a better world.

Sunni Muslim: A servant of Allah (good).

Quaker (follower of George Fox): The best and proper role of human beings in this world is to live in the

Kingdom of God now. This we do by living in and by the light of Christ.

Anglican: To serve and love God and one's fellow man.

Catholic: To feel joy in being loved by God and to love God and others.

Born Again Christian: Be an example of Christ (1 Peter 3:15) towards others in all things.

Anglo-Catholic: To be kind to another person and bring kindness into this world.

Christian: Love God and love each other.

Buddhist: To be kind and compassionate to all life.

Bahá'í: All humans are servants of God, and that is our natural role. Our purpose is to know and love God. We do this by reading the Writings of His Divine Educator, praying to Him, and specifically knowing ourselves and loving/serving others. To love humanity is to love God.

Atheist: To leave the earth better than we came into it.

Christian – Anglican: To be a loving neighbor to all.

Christian – Anglican: To glorify God.

Agnostic: To aid one another.

Eliminative Materialist: An individual exists for the sake of their family and to live according to their role in their ecosystem.

Chinese Buddhist with Taoist Leanings: To become conscious in order to give the universe a window through which to be conscious if you want the "woo-woo" mystic answer. Stewards for the living world around us and would be a more concrete answer.

I don't have a religion: Just do whatever you can without causing unnecessary harm.

Taoist: 'Best' and 'worst' and 'good' and 'bad' etc. imply a one-dimensional scale from one end to the other, and few real-world situations fit into that description. The belief in 'best' and 'worst' causes people a lot of frustration. Perhaps I'm a Taoist because it's one of the few religions I've encountered that acknowledges this problem.

Religious Society of Friends (Quaker): The proper and best role of a human being in this world is to know and glorify God by submitting to a hearing and obeying relationship with Him.

Agnostic Buddhist: To learn how to overcome your own emotions and pride to find the similarities in all of us. To then strive to ensure that every living thing is able to flourish.

Quaker (Christian): Doing good works to improve the lives of others brings the most joy to God and to our own hearts. Not only is it an objective good, it is spiritually nourishing.

Taoist: The one uniquely suited to them.

Jewish, mainly Reform: To experience life.

Daoist: The role that comes naturally when the superficial is discarded and one follows the Dao.

Daoist: To try to be the wisest person you can be.

Open ended, minded: Caretaker. Gardener to teacher, any role that gives.

Eastern Orthodox: Man was created to be a king and a priest: a king because he carries the image of God and rules over the world as a reflection of God's own rule over the world, and a priest because he is to offer the creation back to God as a sacrifice.

Eastern Orthodox: To serve God.

Spiritual: To serve others.

Eastern Orthodox: To help and comfort others.

Daoist: To live, and die.

Undefined: A human guided by strength and compassion.

Taoist: Everything is quite proper.

Sunni Muslim: A modest life.

Buddhist with a splash of Christianity, Taoism and Raja Yoga: I am not sure there is one. I hesitatingly say to rid oneself of suffering and to aid others in ridding themselves of suffering.

Muslim: The primary role should be to live subservient to God. A God fearing person is aware of his duties towards God and other humans.

Buddhist: One who is virtuous, who practices for the welfare of both himself and for others.

Pan-religious (Roman Catholic and Buddhist influences): I do not believe in a 'proper and best role', as I accept all manifestations of aliveness insofar as I can perceive them to exist.

Church of Jesus Christ of Latter-Day Saints: Each of us is sent to this earth to exercise our agency and hopefully choose to follow God's commandments and return to live with Him again. We are tasked with being loving and empathetic and following Christ's example for us. Also, specifically as members of the Church of Jesus Christ of Latter-day Saints, we believe in self-sufficiency. We believe in learning and developing our skills and knowledge so as to be able to support ourselves and contribute in our communities. This includes being able to support one another in our needs and struggles.

Non-denominational Universalist: To become a complete human being with no desire to control others, or to wish others to behave or act in a particular way; to guard against uncontrollable greed, anger and exploitation of material resources and other human beings.

Sikh on paths of Sikhi: Personally, I am not sure that there is a singular best role for every human. Everyone should listen to Divinity within them regularly and follow where their heart and that Divinity guides them.

Jewish (Traditional/Orthodox): To build a better, more just reality for the world at large. For Jewish human beings, that involves the perpetuation and uplifting of the Jewish people.

Jewish (Ultraorthodox / Chabad Lubavitch: To live a lifestyle in accordance with Hashem's will.

8. Do you believe that other religions seek essential truths about humankind and God, and are capable of finding it?

Shia Muslim (Twelver): Yes. I am universalist in some sense, but not in a relativist sense. All religions share aspects of the basic truth, some more straight aimed (like Islam or Zen or Taoism) while other are obfuscated by ideology and culture, but they all (respectively) share aspects of the universal truth.

Evangelical Christian: I believe all humans are spiritual creatures. Each of us has a God-shaped vacuum that can only be filled by a relationship with Jesus. There are elements of truth in all religions because all truth emanates from the one true God.

Shinto: I feel that all religions are the same ideas just interpreted in different ways. I feel though that there are many things that we as mortals cannot know until we pass over.

Baptist: Any religious "truth" found apart from Jesus Christ is a perversion and incapable of saving a person's soul.

Quaker: Yes and yes.

Orthodox Zoroastrian: I do think many other religions seek the truth but I don't think we will ever find it in this world.

Quaker: Yes.

Jewish: Certainly other religions seek essential truths about humankind. That is the nature of religiosity. Whether they are capable of finding those truths is a more difficult question. I do not believe that everyone should be Jewish. I do believe that non-Jews are capable of finding essential truths about humankind and God. I believe that the best way for them to do so is to observe and study the portions of the Torah binding on non-Jews, particularly the Seven Noachide commandments, which we believe are binding on all non-Jews. Adherents to other religions are capable of finding essential truths about humankind and God imperfectly and only to the extent that their religious beliefs are consistent with the Torah.

Taoist when pressed: Yes.

Sunni Muslim (Qadiri Sufi): I think that there is only one truth, and that is Islam and that any other form of truth would be finding Islam through these faiths.

Anglican: All people know some truth about God as we are all made in is image. But Jesus says the He

Himself is the only way to God, and no truth about God can be known except through Him.

Sikh: Yes

Jewish (Agnostic Secular): Yes, most of them at least.

Episcopalian; Anglo-Catholic: Probably, yes. I don't claim to be an expert.

Pentecostal/Calvinist: I believe that followers of other Christian denominations can be saved.

Taoist: Nope.

No religion, just the Tao: Who knows, maybe they will, maybe they won't but I'm sure as hell we won't find the Tao. :D

Multi-Religious: In part. I believe that all ancient revealed religions are valid such as Abrahamic, Vedic, But I do not recognize deism or non-theism as valid religions (such as Taoism and Buddhism). In essence religions means to connect with (a) deity, and if a ritualistic group doesn't do that they are no true religion.

Christian: Yes. This is the purpose of Christ – his death atones for all and all will ultimately be saved, their journey on earth notwithstanding.

Sunni Muslim: Yes.

Quaker (follower of George Fox): Christ is the way, the truth, and the life. No one comes to the Father but by Him. This is as much of a challenge to Christendom as to other religions. All mankind, regardless of religion, are called out of the inventions of man, our sewn-together fig leaves to hide our nakedness of death, to come into the light that comes from the life that is in Christ-the-Word-of-God. We must know what the writer of the book of John said: "And the Word became flesh and tabernacles among us."

Anglican: Yes, but not fully.

Catholic: Yes, but the fullness of truth is preserved within the Catholic Church.

Born Again Christian: No absolutely not. No other religion in the world has anything to do with the truth of God. All other religions are works based systems of self-merit, and not about grace and the Lord God Jesus Christ. They're incapable of finding it unless they repent and believe the Gospel.

Anglo-Catholic: I believe there are many ways to God, but some make it harder to truly find Him. I think there are many paths to heaven but some are the long way up the mountain.

Christian: Yes.

Buddhist: Yes, I believe there are a handful of traditions that are talking about the same thing Zen talks about: Advaita Vedanta and Kashmir Shaivism in Hinduism, Taoism, and mystical teachings around the world.

Bahá'í: All "other religions" are simply the teachings of previous Divine Educators. Ideally humanity would follow the next educator when they appear. All can love and know God and investigate His teachings and serve and learn about humanity. No one is inherently incapable or evil. Anyone may find the truths of creation and the divine. However, Baha'u'llah's teachings are the most recent in the series of divine education and makes the most sense to follow if one desires to connect with God.

Atheist: No, I believe they stick to their indoctrination. If they branched out and studied more than what they believed with an open mind, they wouldn't be so quick to judge another person's religious beliefs because they'll find that they all fundamentally have the same message.

Christian – Anglican: Yes and no. All religions which seek after goodness and beauty (which is basically all of them) contain the seed of truth but not all find the fullness of truth.

Christian – Anglican: Yes.

Agnostic: Yes.

Eliminative Materialist: We don't ascribe any special status to humans over any other living thing, and don't believe in the existence of a God. But certainly other people can reason out true things, for instance we believe that Buddhism is the accurate path to cessation of suffering – if your goal is to end suffering. There's none of us currently practicing that have that goal, but theoretically someone could pass their rite of passage based on that goal.

Chinese Buddhist with Taoist Leanings: Yes, but not all of them. Christian mystics like Meister Eckhart, Brahmans, Sufists all have a tradition similar to seeking enlightenment.

I don't have a religion: Religion isn't about truth.

Taoist: I don't think any religions "seek" any one thing in unison – I think they help groups of people solve contemporary problems. One such problem is seeking the 'truth' of humankind, but it's very hard to define that problem. One could argue that the answer to that must come, by definition, outside the framework of religion. Religion was added to the world by humanity, and the easiest way to understand the world is to remove it again! Or you can decide religion is woven into our social reality because it's some fundamental force expressing itself through us. Golly.

Religious Society of Friends (Quaker): Yes, I think that other religions seek essential truths about humankind, and there are others within those religions who know and serve God. The Friends way of worship, however, provides for a community's gathered listening and hearing to be the primary practice for knowing God's Will.

Agnostic Buddhist: I believe other religions seek essential truths about humankind, yes. That being said, not many do, successfully. No one can answer anything about "God," but only repeat others' stories and beliefs. Many religions have the ability to do great things and many people are able to realize this and live by it. So very many more, however, misrepresent and misconstrue the original thought behind it. If pride and greed can be conquered then I believe all religions have the potential to be great.

Quaker (Christian): Of course! If we are to believe the Lord is omnipotent and all powerful, then we must also believe they can reveal themselves in many ways. So long as love anchors us, all is possible.

Taoist: Some look to humankind, others hold truck with deities. This does not constitute all religious pursuits. What a "religion" is, is a hotly debated topic in academic and clerical circles. As to whether religions are capable of finding an empirical answer to these "truths," yes and no. It is akin to asking someone in love to prove it for all time. It was true when it was true, but it may not hold indefinitely.

Jewish, mainly Reform: Yes.

Daoist: Different religions have different goals and different conceptions of truth and God, but will often provide a path to achieve their specified goals, whether it is understanding rationally the working of the Absolute (Catholicism) or negating one's existence entirely (Buddhism).

Daoist: Nope.

Open ended, minded: Yes, they seek truths, but are incapable of finding any whole truth, for none exists.

Eastern Orthodox: Other religions do seek the truth, but if they do not encounter Christ directly and enter communion with the Orthodox Church they will not only never find the truth, but also never find salvation.

Eastern Orthodox: To some degree, yes.

Spiritual: Organizational religion is ruined by greed. Their beliefs aren't out of scope.

Eastern Orthodox: They may seek it, but they are unable to find it.

Daoist: There are no truths to find.

Undefined: The only people that find it wouldn't have the words to explain it anyway. So it's best to continue leading through personification of great truths.

Taoist: Sure.

Sunni Muslim: I don't know.

Buddhist with a splash of Christianity, Taoism and Raja Yoga: No idea. It might be possible. That question implies there are essential truths. I couldn't tell you if that was true or not.

Muslim: There are two kinds of religions. Those which are revealed and those which are made by humans. All religions in Abrahamic traditions have essentially the same message, that is, believe in God, lots of good deeds, stay away from all kinds of evil, and believe that there will be accountability one day. The other kind of religion where humans have tried to find out the truth by themselves. And these are not capable of finding the whole truth.

Buddhist: I don't pay much attention to other religions and their seeking.

Pan-religious (Roman Catholic and Buddhist influences): Religions don't seek truths because religions do not exist except as constructs in our minds. So, being non-entities, "religions" cannot "seek," only the human beings participating in it. And there are no essential truths to find. Once people realize this, they let go of the search and simply become sensate to the experience of being alive.

Church of Jesus Christ of Latter-Day Saints: Yes. While I believe that the Church of Jesus Christ of Latter-day Saints is God's one true Church on the earth that does not preclude other religions from possessing and seeking out these truths as well.

Non-denominational Universalist: All religions appear to be seeking the ultimate truth but none is venturing to think and operate outside the BOX OF RITUALS AND CUSTOMS each one has inherited and people of their faith have been practicing, which is tantamount to mental indulgence in religious activities. False beliefs and vicarious satisfaction that theirs is the best seems possibly preventing them from moving towards the Ultimate Truth.

Sikh on paths of Sikhi: Yes

Jewish (Traditional/Orthodox): Yes.

Peter Brown

9. Is there life after death, and what does your religion say about it?

Shia Muslim (Twelver): I think the phrase "life after death" is a misnomer and more of a way of trying to comprehend that our souls continue existence in "heaven" or "hell." It is a symbolic thing describing something beyond our comprehension that is real but not familiar. Heaven and Hell are states of the soul: one is a unity with God and the other is a state of the soul becoming purified from its darkness.

Evangelical Christian: Yes! Everyone experiences life after death. Those who have experienced forgiveness for their sins will enjoy life in the presence of the Creator. Those who deny their need of a Savior will spend eternity separated from the Creator and his goodness.

Shinto: Shinto is more concerned with us here now than death. However we do become a mitama (blessed/beautiful spirit) or we have the potential to become a Kami after we move from this world. We believe that death is not the end, instead just another rite of passage.

Baptist: Yes. We will receive new bodies one day, being made pure in soul and flesh, and will dwell in a new heaven and new earth (a newly created realm wherein the material and immaterial will be made one) and dwell with God through the person Jesus.

Quaker: Humans have no way to assess this.

Orthodox Zoroastrian: Avesta says that after death humans "Will unite with their God and reach peace," or Pardis as we call it. But views on this subject vary. Some also believe in a hell and some don't.

Quaker: I don't think so, personally I'm unclear on what my religion says. We don't dwell on it.

Jewish: Yes. A fundamental tenet of my religion is reward and punishment, much of which is deferred to the afterlife. The nature of the afterlife is unclear, and we do not spend a lot of time worrying about that, preferring instead to perfect our lives on earth. But the fundamental nature of the afterlife is that it is pure consequence (reward or punishment) for one's deeds on earth. There is no more ability to act. To the extent that we live our lives in accordance with divine will, our souls in the afterlife will be closer to the bliss of the divine presence. At the same time, we may regret no longer being able to act to improve that position. Also, we believe that at the end of days, the dead will be revived here on earth. The exact nature of that event is also somewhat unclear, and it is not something upon which we dwell, again preferring to perfect our lives in the here and now. But belief in the ultimate revival of the dead here on earth is fundamental.

Taoist when pressed: No one knows, everyone speculates.

Sunni Muslim (Qadiri Sufi): Yes there is, and I want to enter heaven; only the worst of people will enter hell.

Anglican: Yes. Man is ordained a time to life and, after that, judgement. People receive either grace or mercy and live forever in the presence of God, or those who rejected God receive judgement and are punished and eternally cast into outer darkness.

Sikh: Sikhism believes in reincarnation and we all come back in one life form or the other depending the deeds we have done. Important to pray to GOD and do good deeds to get out of the vicious cycle of life and death.

Jewish (Agnostic Secular): Judaism, to my understanding, has multiple, sometimes conflicting positions. Agnosticism says I don't know.

Episcopalian; Anglo-Catholic: My religion says there is, but I'm not so sure about the specifics. I don't think each individual from time immemorial necessarily exists on the same plane or universe but that perhaps there are a limited number of entities who will be present if/when the world ends or transitions.

Pentecostal/Calvinist: Yes, the traditional Protestant view.

Taoist: You'll find out when you get there.

No religion, just the Tao: You live in the Tao, when you die you go back to the Tao. There's no distinction about life and death in particular.

Multi-Religious: Life is eternal. Death is a lie that was created to motivate people to do something with their lives.

Christian: Personally I am conflicted. Our religious tradition generally says yes but details vary broadly.

Sunni Muslim: Yes there is heaven (jannah) and hell (jahannam).

Quaker (follower of George Fox): In the story of the fall, Adam and Eve experienced nakedness because they had lost the covering of the life of God. This is death. God's purpose and work is to bring his creation out of death into life. George Fox stated: "When your minds go forth from the pure spirit of God, and are drawn out from it, there the image of God comes to be lost, in those whose minds go out from the pure, to lust after that which is in the fall, which may appear like truth in the notion; in that nature, out of the truth, lodgeth the enchanter and sorcerer ... For that which joins with the earthly will, goes out from God, and [from] that which is pure; and so makes a place for the enchanter and sorcerer, and the airy spirit, to lodge in; whereby a grave is made for the just, and the partition wall between God and man standing. Death comes to reign, and the grave hath the victory over such ... Dwell in the pure and immortal, and wait upon the living God, to have your hope renewed, and to be renewed again into the image of God, and the image of the devil defaced, and the prince of the air cast out ... So, dwell in the light, and wait upon God to have the image of God renewed; and all come to witness yourselves to be restored by Christ Jesus into the image of God, and to be made by Him like to God, pure, holy, perfect, and righteous. This was witnessed, this is witnessed, and this will be witnessed measurably with thousands, who are growing up out of the fall, and coming up out of the grave." (Epistle 32.) Those who experience and live in this renewal of the image of God within come into the life that that has no end.

Anglican: There is judgement, the resurrection, and the new world to come.

Catholic: There is life after death. There is Hell which is eternal separation from God if somebody dies in a state whereby they are an enemy of God and don't want to be around God. There's Purgatory for those who die in a state of friendship with God but aren't yet pure enough to enjoy the Beatific Vision (Heaven) and as a result go through a process of purification that I personally believe they want to go through. Heaven is a state of perfect and eternal joy where the person enjoys the most intimate possible communion with God and loves God perfectly and feels God's love for him at its peak.

Born Again Christian: Yes, Heaven or Hell.

Anglo-Catholic: Life everlasting. I personally believe death to be a sleep but with or without the love of God to comfort. Hell is to be rejecting of God's love.

Christian: I don't know and it isn't made clear.

Buddhist: There is rebirth. Consciousness continues on in a different body. Enlightenment ends rebirth.

Bahá'í: Yes. Baha'u'llah teaches that we are spiritual souls that reflect in this physical world through the human body. This world is training for the next. We constantly travel through all the worlds of God, getting ever closer to Him, although never reaching Him (would make us equal and as Gods). Heaven and hell are closeness and separation from our Beloved, God, and neither physical places nor levels of the afterlife in the commonly understood sense.

Atheist: Life goes on after a person dies. Is there an afterlife? Not likely, it makes absolutely no sense.

Christian – Anglican: Yes. Those who die reside in Hades (not the Greek pagan version) where they await the coming judgment. Afterwards all of mankind will be separated into the saved and the damned and receive the proper reward or punishment.

Christian – Anglican: My religion says yes, but how would I know?

Agnostic: I'm unsure of life after death. If there is life after death of any kind I'm not sure if we remain conscious. I feel like agnostics would have a wide variety of beliefs on this topic.

Chinese Buddhist with Taoist Leanings: Things keep going on the same way, your children will have their own children, and the brook will keep on flowing. We don't believe consciousness exists in the first place, so the concept of consciousness after death is an absurdity to us. We also believe life is purely the process of birth and death, so a hypothetical eternally continuing sense perception wouldn't be living in any sense.

I don't have a religion: Not important, we all come from the source and are manifestations of the universe.

Taoist: You die when you die. Other things continue living but you just decay or get eaten or both. Death is a part of life, so the question is circular. I find it hard to imagine life arbitrarily starting and stopping, but I'm nowhere close to fathoming what life "outside" being a human would/was/will be like. Taoism itself doesn't set out to answer any of these questions, it just teaches you how to think straight about similar problems, so the above is what I think about life-and-death: so far, anyway!

Religious Society of Friends (Quaker): Friends faith is not speculative; rather it is empirical. As such, it does not promote beliefs which cannot be verified by inward knowledge; speculative belief is regarded as "notional."

Agnostic Buddhist: I don't know. I feel a strange pull toward something. I do not know what or why. As I said, there is no possible way i could ever truly know for sure. I like to believe in reincarnation. I like to believe in being my own judge. But I just do not know. I will do what I can to better myself in the ways I have stated. It is the best i can do, i will cross that bridge once I come to it.

Quaker (Christian): Possibly. In a sense we live on until all memory of us fades. There is no scriptural evidence for a life after death. There is more of an indication that when our body perishes, our soul never dies. Our conscious is what gives us life, and that never dies. The Bible teaches us that we will enter a state of rest until the Lord returns to raise heaven on earth.

Taoist: The religion of Taoism says many and often conflicting things about this. I would contend death is incredibly personal.

Jewish, mainly Reform: You decide.

Daoist: Yes, the human being is composed of multiple different parts that scatter upon death. One part of the soul is reincarnated. One soul receives eternal reward/punishment. One returns to the absolute Dao.

Open ended, minded: Nope. It depends on who you talk to.

Eastern Orthodox: After the fall of man and before the advent of Christ, man (who was created to choose immortality) would die and his soul would be imprisoned in Hades (Hell), where there is no life. After Christ has defeated and destroyed death by the Cross, faithful Orthodox Christians can enter Paradise (Heaven) where they will wait for the Resurrection, while all other individuals go to Hell where they too wait for the Resurrection. At Jesus's second coming, all individuals will be resurrected; some will live eternally in the loving embrace of God (the Kingdom of God) and others will live eternally in tormenting fire (Gehenna), which is also called the second death. As such, the "first death" is only a temporary separation of the body and the soul, for all people.

Eastern Orthodox: Yes. Those who worship the Trinity and live according to the teachings of the faith, they will life eternally in spirit, and if not, spend eternity in total separation from God.

Spiritual: No.

Eastern Orthodox: Yes. One is aware after death. No other dogma exists.

Daoist: Yes. Death isn't life. Death is death.

Undefined: There might be. But you won't find out until the end of the story anyway. We might as well continue down our paths without any doubts.

Taoist: I don't think that Taoism says much about this. I tend to believe that, similarly to a psychedelic experience, dying can greatly expand time. Maybe a million years in a second. Who knows?

Sunni Muslim: Yes, heaven or hell.

Buddhist with a splash of Christianity, Taoism and Raja Yoga: I don't know. Buddhist may tell you after death we are reborn after death until we all achieve enlightenment.

Muslim: Basically this world is created as a test for humans. Those will purify their hearts will, as a reward, be able to live forever with unlimited rewards. Most of the Quran talks about life after death.

Buddhist: Strictly speaking Buddhists do not believe in death.

Pan-religious (Roman Catholic and Buddhist influences): The separation or duality between life and death is an illusion.

Church of Jesus Christ of Latter-Day Saints: Yes, there is life after death. We are all spiritual beings. We existed before this world and will exist after it. We came to this world and obtained a physical body; after our physical bodies die, our spirits live on and, through Christ's atonement, will eventually be reunited with our perfected physical forms through resurrection at the last days. Our religion specifically believes that there are degrees of glory in the post-mortal life. All these degrees of glory would still be considered "heaven" as the term is more commonly used. We believe that Hell also exists but that it is quite difficult to "earn" your spot there. Hell, which we refer to as "Outer Darkness" is where Satan and the Sons of Perdition will reside. In order to go to Hell, one must have a knowledge of God the Father and deny Him. One's position in the degrees of glory is related to one's faithfulness on this earth. We also believe that those who did not have an opportunity during their lifetimes to hear the teachings of the Church and choose of him or herself to accept them, will have that opportunity in the afterlife.

Non-denominational Universalist: One can understand LIFE AFTER DEATH only when he/she can free him/herself from all types of bondage, be it family, friends, relatives, materialistic attachments and above all one's Life Itself. Our religion commands that attainment of blissful state is possible only when learns to conduct and behave like a dead person when is living this life physically.

Sikh on paths of Sikhi: Sure there are all sorts of things that can happen. After all, human or not, all are a part of The One Force. Personally I feel that Sikhi stresses to focus on the present. What will be will be, but what are you doing right now!?

Jewish (Traditional/Orthodox): Yes, but Judaism cautions against any certainty as to what the "world to come" actually involves.

Jewish (Ultraorthodox / Chabad Lubavitch): Yes. The soul exists forever and delights in Hashem's glory.

Peter Brown

10.   Is your religion based on scripture, and if so, what is that scripture and by whom was it written or transmitted?

Shia Muslim (Twelver): Yes, The Qur'an, received by the prophet Muhammad. Revealed progressively over 23 years, it was transmitted by speech; opinions on when it was written down vary between Sunnis and Shias.

Evangelical Christian: Yes it is based on the Hebrew Bible (the Old Testament) and the New Testament. We believe it to be inspired and authoritative and the only perfect guide for faith, doctrine and conduct.

Shinto: There is no scripture in Shinto.

Baptist: The scripture we use is made up of the 66 books of the Bible. It was written by 40+ men over a roughly 2000 year period of time, superintended in its authorship and protected in its preservation by the Holy Spirit.

Quaker: Limited Christian Gospel: Matthew, Mark, Luke and John. To a more limited extent Genesis and Exodus.

Orthodox Zoroastrian: Avesta. Zarathustra /Zoroaster / Zartošt.

Quaker: Not really. George Fox said some rad stuff. Christ did, as well.

Jewish: Yes, it is based on the Torah. The Written Torah is the Five Books of Moses (Genesis, Exodus, Leviticus, Numbers and Deuteronomy). We also believe in an Oral Torah that explains the Written Torah. The Oral Torah has never been completely written down, but is codified to some extent in the Tanach (Bible, basically what Christians refer to as the "Old Testament" although ordered differently) and the Talmud (written down in the first few hundred years of the Common Era). We believe that God dictated the Written Torah letter by letter to Moses and also explained the Oral Torah to him 3331 years ago. It was then transmitted generation to generation from Moses to Joshua to the early Elders of Israel, to the Prophets (as described in the Tanach) to the Men of the Great Assembly (around 2500 years ago), then later to the Tannaim ("Teachers" who lived from a couple hundred years before the Common Era to about the year 200 in the Common Era), to the "Amoraim" ("Expounders", who lived from the 200s to the 400s), to the "Savoraim" ("Reasoners", who lived in the 500s), to the "Gaonim" ("Geniuses", who lived in the 600s to the 900s), to the "Rishonim" (the "first ones", who lived from the 1000s to the 1500s), to the "Acharonim" (the "last ones", who lived from the 1500s to present times).

Taoist when pressed: Primarily the Daodejing, a book about how we aren't going to find any answers by reading a book.

Sunni Muslim (Qadiri Sufi): Quran which is written as well as orally transmitted, and the Hadith which were first orally transmitted.

Anglican: Yes. The Old Testament written by various authors. Kings, Prophets, etc. Written in Hebrew and meticulously copied by the priests and kings. The New Testament written by eyewitnesses and friends of Jesus, written in Greek and highly attested to despite the persecution of the early church. Very difficult but tenacious transmission history.

Sikh: Yes the "ADI GRANTH" the Guru Granth Sahib is the scripture of Sikh religion. It was written in Gurmukhi, compiled and written by Guru Arjun Dev ji (the 5th Guru Ji).

Jewish (Agnostic Secular): Yes. The T.N.KH., Torah Neviim Ktuvim, the Jewish Bible, a compilation of myths, history, poems and laws, of which the Torah, which includes probably myths and laws, is believed to have been given by God to Moses on Mount Sinai in the latter half of the 2nd millennium BC, but which probably was written, together with the rest of the Bible, by multiple authors throughout the 1st millennium BC.

Also, kind of, the Mishna, a compilation of Oral traditions and laws written by rabbis/sages in the first centuries AD.

Episcopalian; Anglo-Catholic: Yes, my religion is based scripturally on the Bible and more loosely on other church writings. The Bible is said to be the word of God transmitted through human prophets and thus is an interpretation of the world of God by and for humans, including subsequent editing by major figures of the historical church.

Pentecostal/Calvinist: The Bible written by men and inspired by God.

Taoist: The Big Lebowski.

No religion, just the Tao: It began with the Tao Te Ching, said to have been written approximately 2,000 years ago by a court official named Lao Zi, but the religion isn't based on it, it's based on experiences of past Taoists till the present.

Multi-Religious: I accept most revealed scriptures as true. I accept some newer channeled texts as a gateway to truth. I accept some fictional works as religiously relevant and pointing towards the gateway of truth.

Christian: Yes – God inspired humans to write the Hebrew Bible and the New Testament. I do think it is possible for continuing revelations to be communicated but the Bible is the "core" of our practices and the holy book of the church.

Sunni Muslim: Not necessarily.

Quaker (follower of George Fox): My faith is not interchangeable with religion. It is based on the continued experience of hearing and following the voice of God. Scripture, i.e. the Bible, is the testimony that points to a living experience of Christ, the Word of God, as the source of life. The scriptures were written by men who also experienced hearing and following the voice of God. The Bible is neither infallible nor inerrant. It contains accidental as well as deliberate mistranslations or bending of meaning to fit pet theological positions. It is a book that has passed through significant changes of language and conceptual understanding relevant to one language but not found in another language. However it is a worthy testimony of those who have walked this road before I did.

Anglican: The Christian Bible. It is written by human hands by the direct inspiration of God.

Catholic: Yes, sort of. There's the Bible. It was written by several authors but all was inspired by the Holy Spirit. Scripture is not the sole source of authority.

Born Again Christian: 2 Peter 1:20-21. Knowing this first, that no prophecy of the scripture is of any private interpretation. For the prophecy came not in old time by the will of man: but holy men of God spake as they were moved by the Holy Ghost.

Anglo-Catholic: I would say the Bible, but some parts can only be taken as a metaphor for how to live. I think the church has to help with translation sometimes as the lay people aren't studied in ancient languages or the complex histories.

Christian: Bible.

Buddhist: It depends on the tradition within Buddhism. Theravadin and Mahayana Buddhists tend to emphasize different scriptures, so there is no one single holy book all Buddhists agree on, as far as I know. I personally prefer books that have the collected talks of old Chinese Zen masters, but Zen is traditionally based on scriptures like the Diamond Sutra, Mahaparinirvana Sutra, and the Lankavatara Sutra.

Bahá'í: Written by Baha'u'llah. The Bab's Writings are also considered authoritative unless overwritten by Baha'u'llah (essentially all laws were overwritten). Many books and tablets www.bahai.org. Writings of other Divine Educators (Bible, Quran, etc.) are Divine although authenticity is not necessarily the same as Baha'u'llah's, which were written by hand or taken down by a secretary.

Atheist: Nope.

Christian – Anglican: Yes. Anglicanism prides itself on having nothing "repugnant to the Word of God," which is the Bible. The most common Anglican translation is the King James Bible, which is the foundation of modern English. It was written by multiple authors of ancient Israel and beyond who were all guided by the Holy Spirit into recording profound theological truths.

Christian – Anglican: The Bible. It was decided by the early church.

Agnostic: No.

Eliminative Materialist: Not based on scripture. The closest equivalent would be when people have written down their beliefs after going through their rite of passage.

Chinese Buddhist with Taoist Leanings: Yes and no; there are Buddhist scriptures but it was an oral tradition for a long enough time that when it was finally written down it diverged into enough different interpretations to render them halfway irrelevant. The practices are more important in many ways.

I don't have a religion: I don't have a religion.

Taoist: Taoism, as we know it, is rooted almost completely in a single book: the Tao Te Ching, said to be written by Laozi, sometime before the 7th century. Details of the date and authorship are disputed, but not hugely. English translations didn't surface until the 19th century. There have been disputes that some translations lose the original intent, but that's a fact of life with translations.

Religious Society of Friends (Quaker): Friends belief is based on inward experience, and it is corroborated by Scripture (Bible) in both Testaments. The Book of John is particularly cherished by Friends.

Agnostic Buddhist: No, not my personal beliefs. Buddhism has. It has had many transcriptions, writers, etc. There really isn't just one book. There are many. I read and adored a book called "Buddhist Scriptures" by

Edward Conze. It is a collection of some of the more prominent stories from different sources.

Quaker (Christian): Yes. We base our faith primarily on the New Testament of the Holy Bible. There are many authors who are disputed.

Taoist: More orthopraxy than orthodoxy. However, there is a Taoist canon and a few classic Taoist scholars (i.e. Lao Tzu, Chuang Tzu, The 7 Drunken Sages) that form much of the literary basis of the religion.

Jewish, mainly Reform: The Old Testament, said to chronicle true stories of our forefathers. This may be oral tradition convoluted by thousands of years of man.

Daoist: Scripture is important, but not the only factor. All Daoist sects do share the common foundation of the DDJ, albeit with various differing interpretations.

Daoist: There are books. But ultimately "you have to figure it out for yourself" is the guiding principle.

Open ended, minded: I have borrowed from many different scriptures and writings over my life. None are more valuable than the other, and each offers insight and understanding.

Eastern Orthodox: Orthodox Christianity is principally based on the Bible, although the Bible itself is only one part (but the main part) of the tradition transmitted from the apostles to now. The Bible is a collection of 66 inspired books (plus others called anagignoskomena or "profitable to read"), almost all of which have different authors, audiences, and literary styles. The compilation of 66 books was finally accepted universally in the 6th century, with the Revelation of St. John being the last accepted book.

Eastern Orthodox: Yes, In fact, the founders wrote most of it, and later church fathers drew theological conclusions from it. Our scripture was later canonized by the church.

Spiritual: No.

Eastern Orthodox: Not all of the faith is based on scripture. The faith is also based on the Church.

Daoist: Lao-tzu. Chaung-Tzu.

Undefined: Scripture written in the breeze flowing through a Willow tree. Scripture on the cold dew resting on the green grass. Scripture in the touch of a loved one. Scripture in the pain of loss. Scripture in the malicious deeds of a neighbor. Scripture in the apologies of your father's killer. Scripture never written, but always read off the face of every atom in this universe.

Taoist: It's hard to say if it's based on the Tao Te Ching or not. I tend to think that it's older than that. Also, the author Lao Tzu simply means old wise man so it probably was not a historical character.

Sunni Muslim: Originally transmitted orally, then compiled by the third caliph, Uthman.

Buddhist with a splash of Christianity, Taoism and Raja Yoga: Kind of. The scripture offers advice and warnings. But I would say Buddhism is based on practice: virtue, meditation, and discernment. The cannon's history is interesting; there are many different schools that will tell what is and what isn't accepted. Pretty much all schools agree that the Pali canon is accepted. It was memorized by one of the Buddha's students. It was then transmitted orally for a few hundred years, I think, and then written down.

Muslim: Islam is based on Quran. Quran was revealed to Muhammad PBUH during a period of 23 years. He was unlettered so whenever he received revelation, he would ask his companions to write it down.

Buddhist: The Buddhist canon or tipitaka was transmitted orally for a few hundred years until it was committed to text by the Buddhist council.

Pan-religious (Roman Catholic and Buddhist influences): I believe that words are limited and limiting symbols. Metaphysical truth is best experienced in states of wordlessness. Silence does not require interpersonal transmission.

Church of Jesus Christ of Latter-Day Saints: Our Church is not strictly based on scripture, but is led by Jesus Christ. We believe the Bible to be the word of God as far as it is translated correctly. We also believe the Book of Mormon to be the word of God. We believe that study of these scriptures, which are inspired by God and teach us of Him and how we should live our lives is essential. The Bible and Book of Mormon were transmitted by God through his prophets and other holy men. Each of these books was written by holy prophets and apostles from ancient times, and translated in modern days for our access to the richness of their teachings.

Non-denominational Universalist: Yes – for details, see Answer to Question 5 above.

Sikh on paths of Sikhi: Kind of. In addition to 'scripture', the religion is based on how the values written are manifested in the Guru Khalsa Panth. How do real people following the path of Sikhi behave with Love and how can we learn from those stories. Mentioned earlier, the Guru Granth Sahib is a compilation of Divine-inspired words written in bulk by the 10 Sikh Gurus but also include words of poets of other religions whose philosophy aligned with Guru Nanak Sahib.

Jewish (Traditional/Orthodox): Answered above: our scripture is the Tanach (Five Books of Moses, Prophetic Books, Holy Writings) and the Oral Law (Talmud) consisting of Mishna and Gmorah.

Jewish (Ultraorthodox / Chabad Lubavitch): Yes answered   above.

Peter Brown

11. Should scripture be understood literally, allegorically, metaphorically or otherwise?

Shia Muslim (Twelver): There are about 8 layers of interpretation of which a piece of scripture exists, and reading it literally is only one of those.

Evangelical Christian: It all depends on the kind of literature it was to begin with. History books are to be taken literally. Poetic books and parables are to be taken symbolically. The context of the author's life and culture and the author's intent is key to understanding how to apply the Scriptures.

Shinto: I believe everyone should make their own choices. If someone must use scripture, it should never be referred to literally.

Baptist: Context is key. The Bible is good about keying its reader into the type of literature at play (narrative, poetry, parable, allegory, etc.).

Orthodox Zoroastrian: Metaphorically.

Quaker: Otherwise.

Jewish: All of the above and more. Judaism holds that Scripture can be understood on four fundamental levels: (1) "pshat" or literal meaning; (2) "drash" or allegorical/metaphorical meaning; (3) "Remez" or prophetic meaning; and (4) "Sod" or secret, mystical meaning.

Taoist when pressed: Depends on the scripture.

Sunni Muslim (Qadiri Sufi): "It is He Who has sent down to you (Muhammad وسلم عليه الله صلى) the Book (this Qur'aan). In it are Verses that are entirely clear, they are the foundations of the Book [and those are the Verses of Al-Ahkaam (commandments), Al-Faraa'id (obligatory duties) and Al-Hudood (laws for the punishment of thieves, adulterers)]; and others not entirely clear. So as for those in whose hearts there is a deviation (from the truth) they follow that which is not entirely clear thereof, seeking Al-Fitnah (polytheism and trials), and seeking for its hidden meanings, but none knows its hidden meanings save Allah. And those who are firmly grounded in knowledge say: "We believe in it; the whole of it (clear and unclear Verses) are from our Lord. And none receive admonition except men of understanding." [Aal 'Imraan 3:7.]

Anglican: Literally. Taking into account context.

Sikh: Literally.

Jewish (Agnostic Secular): Judaism, in the Talmud and Mishna, sometimes thinks literally, allowing loopholes, and sometimes expands scripture to be stricter. I am not sure personally if it should be understood at all, maybe as a general moral statement, maybe literally sometimes.

Episcopalian; Anglo-Catholic: I think scripture should primarily be understood metaphorically as a literary work designed to encompass important teaching and background. However there are many ways to view Scripture and it calls for many strategies to understand it fully.

Pentecostal/Calvinist: Mostly literally.

Taoist: Metaphorically.

No religion, just the Tao: "The Tao that can be spoken of is not the true Tao" TTC ch.1.

Multi-Religious: We can only talk peacefully about our understanding of scripture by following the literal plain meanings. Any esoteric understanding of scripture is intended to be revealed to individuals only and not as a basis for discussion.

Christian: It is a library, really: depends on the book!

Sunni Muslim: Allegorically.

Quaker (follower of George Fox): The scriptures cannot be understood without the reader being led by the same spirit that inspired the writers. There are many layers of understanding that can be derived poetically, literally, allegorically, and metaphorically.

Anglican: Depending on the genre of the book in question.

Catholic: All three.

Born Again Christian: It is the literal words of the living God, and it contains allegory, metaphor, and direct truth. It has only one interpretation and many applications

Anglo-Catholic: Some parts should be interpreted as metaphors (ex. Adam and Eve), and some parts literally (ex. Jesus healing the blind or being born of the Virgin Mary).

Christian: As a narrative story.

Buddhist: It depends on the text you are reading. And sometimes different approaches may be needed even within the same text.

Bahá'í: Those before Baha'u'llah's should be understood metaphorically in most cases. Baha'u'llah has said that in this Dispensation teachings are given clearly, although in many cases with examples meant to give broader meaning. Scripture is to be understood as authentic and not changeable by human beings.

Atheist: I think it needs to be studied literally and accepted metaphorically. Instead of picking and choosing to shove down another person's life, a believer should show their faith by their own actions.

Christian – Anglican: The Bible is not a single monolith but a collection of multiple books of multiple genres and authors. The Book of Genesis is clearly allegorical whereas the Gospel of Mark is clearly literal. All the books of the Bible are truthful theologically, if not necessarily useful as a scientific or history textbook. Each book of the Bible needs to be evaluated on its own basis. Any sweeping judgment of taking "the Bible" literally or metaphorically is an uneducated judgment.

Christian – Anglican: All three.

Agnostic: All three, which can make things difficult, but I feel like all three are useful.

Eliminative Materialist: The aforementioned written accounts of rites of passage are taken as philosophical arguments regarding the nature of the universe. They are entirely up for debate.

Chinese Buddhist with Taoist Leanings: Yes to all.

I don't have a religion: It doesn't matter because they are false any way you read them.

Taoist: The text opens with a sentence pointing out that the text itself should not be taken literally, and claims that the concept of the Tao can't be captured in writing at all – then proceeds to try to build from there. The honesty is refreshing, and sets the tone well. To answer the question, I'd say that places it squarely in "otherwise".

Religious Society of Friends (Quaker): Scripture must be read in the same Spirit in which it was written to be rightly understood.

Agnostic Buddhist: I suppose that is up to the person. Metaphors and allegory are much easier to use in each other's lives. I do not think all should be taken literally. If so, the next coming of Buddha will be to a king and queen. The queen will walk into the forest and give birth. Buddha will be able to walk and talk as soon as he is out, ha ha. I'm sorry ... but even I cannot take that literally. Religion should be a personal interpretation. I wish I could say that it will always and 100% be the best interpretation. I am not that foolish. I know it will be taken every single way, even the most backwards of ways. The one thing I can say I love about Buddhism most is it is a pretty universal teaching of compassion and acceptance. Most Buddhists I have met have not held their judgement and pride in the foreground. I cannot say that about any other religion that I have knowledge of, unfortunately.

Quaker (Christian): I look at the Bible as more of a library. I don't believe it is a unified text, more like a collections of lessons that teach us to be better people.

Taoist: There is virtually no way to take a scripture literally. The closest approximation would be the Quran, but even there the literal understanding is usually tempered with other cultural influences.

Jewish, mainly Reform: Allegorically.

Daoist: Different sects have different interpretations, but scripture must always be approached holistically and within context.

Daoist: It depends on the book; there are lots and lots of them.

Open ended, minded: Depends totally on the context.

Eastern Orthodox: Scripture should be understood in light of the four gospels (Matthew, Mark, Luke, John) and of the Church's own tradition, often making the line between "literal", "allegorical" and "metaphorical" blurry. We have to understand that the scriptures are like the icons used in Orthodox tradition: they depict events using unrealistic colors and strange perspectives, but only to open us to the reality of the Kingdom of God and express the mystery of Christ in a language of prayer and contemplation rather than with scientific realism. The same could be said about the scriptures. This is not to take into account that some books are outright recognized as poetic works (Song of Songs, Job, for instance).

Eastern Orthodox: All of the above.

Spiritual: Metaphorically.

Eastern Orthodox: Otherwise.

Daoist: To be trapped in the literal is to miss the starting gun.

Undefined: Experientially.

Taoist: Certainly not literally, I'm not sure about the difference between allegorical and metaphorical.

Sunni Muslim: Metaphorically.

Buddhist with a splash of Christianity, Taoism and Raja Yoga: I suppose it can be any, all or none. It should all always be tested. If it fails your experiential test then either adapt your perspective, or drop it for now.

Muslim: It should be read as it was intended to be read by the creator of that scripture. Quran is a very simple and straightforward book. There are no puzzle or riddles. However, the context is important.

Peter Brown

Buddhist: There are cases where the scripture speaks literally, allegorically, and metaphorically.

Pan-religious (Roman Catholic and Buddhist influences): Scripture should be understood as a collection of words, and words should be understood as constructions of imagination.

Church of Jesus Christ of Latter-Day Saints: The scriptures are understood in a multitude of different ways depending upon the passages which one is reading. God utilized many devices to expound His teachings. To that extent, the answer to your question is situation specific. Should we take literally an eye for an eye, I think not. Though I believe that justice in the afterlife will be served. But do I believe we should not commit adultery, literally? Yes.

Non-denominational Universalist: Those who wrote scriptures did so when they were in touch with the INFINITE POWER. True understanding of scriptures will come only to that person who raises him/herself to that level where he/she remains in touch with the Infinite/Supreme Power.

Sikh on paths of Sikhi: Yes.

Jewish (Traditional/Orthodox): All of the above.

Jewish (Ultraorthodox / Chabad Lubavitch): According to the   oral   tradition.

12.   What is God?

Shia Muslim (Twelver): An ineffable, absolute unity, a universal intellect and singular point on which the universe manifests. God is beyond the universe but is ever-present (not in a material sense).

Evangelical Christian: God is the Divine Creator who is the all knowing, all present and all powerful source of life and truth who desires a relationship with all humanity.

Shinto: 'God' is the universal energy that exists within all things including ourselves.

Baptist: The Creator of all things.

Orthodox Zoroastrian: Knowledge and knowledge giver. Peace and peace giver. Light and light giver.

Quaker: An enlightened consciousness, as guided by a path towards equality

Jewish: The Creator of the Universe and the Primary Cause of all existence who is perfect in every manner of existence. That is Maimonides' first of thirteen principles of the Jewish faith.

Taoist when pressed: Me, you, and everything else. Oneness.

Sunni Muslim (Qadiri Sufi): The being who created everything, He exists outside of all time and space and everything is of His creation. He has no physical form that we can comprehend and cannot be bound by human logic.

Anglican: The creator and sustainer of all things. The eternal God.

Sikh: The Divine source; One God the Creator, Preserver and Destroyer. The Father/Mother of all and we are all his children.

Jewish (Agnostic Secular): A conscious entity which exists outside of this physical world and universe (maybe within it in some circumstances – no, I am not talking about Jesus) and which influenced it in some way or which influences people's consciousness after death.

Episcopalian; Anglo-Catholic: God is an idea or being, probably not a literal physical person, who holds tremendous power and who oversees, potentially indirectly, the working space of the universe, the creation of the universe (and perhaps other universes), and the overall execution of a plan of creation.

Pentecostal/Calvinist: Incomprehensible, good, creator.

Taoist: A higher power.

No religion, just the Tao: Who knows, but I'm pretty sure it's not the Tao.

Multi-Religious: Deity is not a what but a who.

Christian: Being, consciousness, bliss as David Bentley Hart might say.

Sunni Muslim: He is the creator of all life, the world, and mankind.

Quaker (follower of George Fox): God is not a "what" but a "who." He created all things and is calling all back into the order of creation. This is not dependent upon any particular theology of creation – evolution or creationism. He is the source of life, the source of right relationship with all created order.

Anglican: Triune.

Catholic: Love. (Most essentially at least.)

Born Again Christian: John 4:24, God is a Spirit: and they that worship Him must worship Him in spirit and in truth.

Anglo-Catholic: The relationship between the trinity and love.

Christian: Love.

Buddhist: Beyond human comprehension. That which nothing greater can be conceived, to paraphrase Anselm. There is no suffering, desire, or questions. Buddhists do not believe in a creator God but I think Nirvana can be thought as something similar to God.

Bahá'í: Creator, perfect being with all spiritual qualities. Loving to humanity. Unknowable to humanity.

Atheist: Different things to different people. To me, God is a security blanket that protects people from the unknown, gives people a crutch to lean on for places they're weak, and a scapegoat to hide behind while they judge people for things that are different to them.

Christian – Anglican: Father, Son and Holy Spirit, who was and is and is to come.

Christian – Anglican: The grounding of all being.

Agnostic: Everything.

Eliminative Materialist: We believe existence requires definition, and that it is impossible to construct a coherent definition of a God, largely because we don't believe consciousness or spirit exists. As a result, we don't merely believe God doesn't exist (which would imply it could potentially exist if the circumstances were different), we believe a God is incapable of existence.

Chinese Buddhist with Taoist Leanings: The guiding intelligence of the universe that creates everything and is beyond scientific explanation (for now). I feel that the anthropomorphic dude in the clouds thing just feels like vain bullshit from a self-obsessed species.

I don't have a religion: A human invention based on the assumption of transcendent cognition or the more rational concepts addicted to a higher power.

Taoist: The word people use when they're missing part of the answer. Like an 'x' in an equation.

Religious Society of Friends (Quaker): God is the Creator, who speaks to humankind, which is made in His image.

Agnostic Buddhist: "God", to me, is not a person or great creator. "God" is what I strive to be. It is a state of being that is reached through many lives and learning. It is the ultimate accomplishment to strive to reach. When we have finally learned everything we are meant to learn we become one with all before and after that have reached that level of enlightenment.

Quaker (Christian): God is love.

Taoist: Not a noun, more an adjective.

Jewish, mainly Reform: Everything.

Daoist: I don't know.

Daoist: God doesn't exist.

Open ended, minded: A word. Me. You. Everything. Nothing.

Eastern Orthodox: God is the Creator of all things, the principle without principles, who has revealed Himself as Love, Justice, Compassion, Mercy...

Eastern Orthodox: The very creator of the entire universe and whom we serve (but willingly)

Spiritual: It is all of us realizing our best self.

Eastern Orthodox: God is the Creator of all things, visible and invisible.

Daoist: The beginning and the end.

Undefined: The space in between the end and the beginning of time.

Taoist: The universe, everything.

Sunni Muslim: The most high entity.

Buddhist with a splash of Christianity, Taoism and Raja Yoga: I have no idea. What does God mean?

Muslim: He is Allah, [who is] One. Allah is the Eternal Refuge. He neither begets nor is born, nor is there to Him any equivalent.

Buddhist: Buddhism doesn't have a creator God or divine source. It does have a complex cosmology with Gods, devas, brahmas and others but these play no role in our deliverance.

Pan-religious (Roman Catholic and Buddhist influences): Whatever is.

Church of Jesus Christ of Latter-Day Saints: God is our Father in Heaven, the creator of our spiritual forms and of everything in this world. He loves us and knows us individually. He has a body of flesh and blood.

Non-denominational Universalist: You cannot study or explain God – you have to dissolve into It.

Sikh on paths of Sikhi: A Singular Divine Force, Truth, Creative Being, Without Fear or Enmity, Timeless, Without Form, Self-Existent.

Jewish (Traditional/Orthodox): God is what is.

Jewish (Ultraorthodox / Chabad Lubavitch): A being that always existed. The source of all existence.

13.   Do you speak to God, does God speak to you in some sense, and what is the best path to achieve awareness of God?

Shia Muslim (Twelver): Does God speak to me? not in my experience. The best path is one of absolute devotion and focus; as in Hinduism, we have many rituals (like our daily Salat) that help us over time to be more in tune with the word as it really is.

Evangelical Christian: Reading the Scriptures is the way God speaks to me. I also sense God's guidance and desire for my life through the still small voice of conscience. I communicate to God through prayer.

Shinto: I can speak to the Kami at any time. There is no prerequisite to speak to Gods. We must just listen. Because all people on earth have the energy of God, our own thoughts are often those that are meant to guide us.

Baptist: I pray to God, but He does not answer back in a discernable voice. That said, He does change my heart and guide me through His written word (which I believe contains all that I need in order to know him).

Orthodox Zoroastrian: I do. Maybe God does speak to me but I won't listen. You can't; there's a reason why it's called "faith".

Quaker: Community. If God is in us all, God can be best found in an assemblage.

Jewish: I speak to God through prayer. God does not speak directly to me since we believe that, for the time being, prophecy ceased to exist about 2500 years ago. However, God speaks to me in a sense through the Torah, both the Written Torah and the essentially infinite Oral Torah. The best path to achieve awareness of God is to observe and study the Torah.

Taoist when pressed: "Know thyself".

Sunni Muslim (Qadiri Sufi): I pray to God and I feel that my prayers are answered

Anglican: God speaks to us by the Bible. We are to come to God and speak to Him in prayer. Understanding His word is a good path to awareness of God.

Sikh: I believe than we can speak to GOD, you hear from God with answered prayers, your gut instinct. Paths to God's Awareness is developing spiritual awareness via meditation, prayers and obedience.

Jewish (Agnostic Secular): Sometimes I speak to God in hope that He is there and hears me.

Episcopalian; Anglo-Catholic: I am a musician and my primary interaction with God is through music. To a lesser extent, worship, prayer, and meditation are all means to draw nearer to God and have conversations with them. I don't always consciously perceive my interactions with God, but I believe through practice I can become more aware and more connected with God.

Pentecostal/Calvinist: Yes, yes, prayer and reading the Bible.

Taoist: Look around in nature and anything on this earth long enough and it will speak.

No religion, just the Tao: There's no distinction between God and human in the Tao, I am the Tao, the God is the Tao, I am him he is me and the Tao is both of us, we just merely differ in what part of the Tao is us.

Multi-Religious: There are several revealed ways to connect/communicate with Deity. And those are equally valid.

Christian: Contemplation, meditation, silence help as disciplines. As a Christian I believe I see Christ's face in all but especially the most afflicted among us. I do pray.

Sunni Muslim: Pray to Him five times a day.

Quaker (follower of George Fox): God is the Creator who speaks to people demanding a response. It is the voice of God that exercises our consciences and informs our understanding. It requires an "achievement" to isolate ourselves from God who calls, "Adam, Adam, where are you? Who told you you were naked? Have you disobeyed My voice?"

Anglican: Prayer.

Catholic: Yes. The best path.... there's no one best path except for maybe Communion.

Born Again Christian: I do regularly, and He does with me all the time. The best way to get there is to believe on the Lord Jesus Christ and thou shalt be saved, and the indwelling of the Spirit of God will direct you.

Anglo-Catholic: Through prayer, yes.

Christian: I speak to God in prayer and He speaks to me in meditation, through other people and in many ways. To achieve awareness confess sins and repair wrongdoing, in a state of right relationship we can receive God.

Buddhist: My theological beliefs are outside the scope of Buddhism because the Buddha did not teach theological navel gazing and thought it could distract one from the path. I have had weird experiences of synchronicity that have at times felt like something greater was trying to communicate with me or lure me in a specific direction, but I can never know for certain. I think different people need different paths and there is no best path, but if there is a God I believe Hinduism is most accurate, theologically, and has numerous prescribed practices to fit different needs in order to achieve awareness of God.

Bahá'í: Prayer is communion with God. We also worship by prayer, service, work, etc. God can confirm us in what we do and guide us, although we can never really know when He is doing this.

Atheist: While searching, I tried but was never answered literally or metaphorically.

Christian – Anglican: I speak to God through prayer and while I don't hear physical words back, I do feel that He communicates to me in other means, such as people. The best path to achieve awareness of God is still, silent prayer and corporate worship.

Christian – Anglican: God is a verb. Awareness of God is best achieved through living its will as best as you can understand it.

Agnostic: None of that at the moment. I wish I could.

Eliminative Materialist: Not applicable.

Chinese Buddhist with Taoist Leanings: Meditation.

I don't have a religion: I don't have conversations with things that don't exist.

Taoist: I think these questions are tailored to a preconceived idea of how to parse reality. They seem meaningless to me.

Religious Society of Friends (Quaker): Prayer is opening one's heart to receive knowledge of God and Christ. The best path to achieve awareness of God is to love truth and act accordingly.

Agnostic Buddhist: In a sense, I suppose so. God is in the sacrifices I make for others. God is my conscience telling me what I should do instead of what is easiest. I feel God in the joy I give to others when I surprise them. God is in compassion.

Quaker (Christian): I speak to God, and in His own mysterious ways He speaks to me. We believe as Quakers that group silence will allow God to speak directly to a member of the congregation and reveal his message to us. Silent contemplation of God and the self is the best way to achieve this.

Taoist: This is a non sequitur to following the Tao.

Jewish, mainly Reform: Sometimes I pray. Sometimes I see larger purpose. My perspective on natural order encourages my faith.

Daoist: God is not a person. The Dao can be experienced through non-doing and living a life of simplicity.

Daoist: Daoism doesn't believe in the Abrahamic God. The fact that you assume that all religions do, just shows how little you know about the world's different spiritual traditions.

Open ended, minded: Yes, no, gardening.

Eastern Orthodox: We speak to God through prayer, and God speaks to us through everything that is holy – whether the Bible, the sacraments, or the whole creation itself. The best path to achieve awareness of God is to practice prayer, fasting, and charity to the best of one's abilities, and partake of the Eucharist whenever possible.

Eastern Orthodox: Hesychasm can be a good way. The goal of Christian Life is Theosis.

Spiritual: I seek inner peace which will bring us closest to our "God".

Eastern Orthodox: Yes. Yes. Prayer.

Daoist: That God is just your subconscious talking to itself.

Undefined: My morals speak to me. My personal experiences personified, speak to me.

Taoist: The psychedelic experience, for sure. Then you don't need to believe. Then you "know".

Sunni Muslim: No.

Buddhist with a splash of Christianity, Taoism and Raja Yoga: Again depends on what you mean by God ha ha. I don't think it is very important.

Muslim: God speaks to us through Quran (and previous scriptures such as Torah, Psalms etc.). Quran is the best and most reliable way to achieve awareness and recognition of God. For example God introduces Himself in the start of Quran as utmost compassionate and merciful. All praises and gratefulness is due Him as He is the Lord (and Creator) of the universes.

Buddhist: Again, Buddhism doesn't have a God that is worshipped or petitioned for intercession.

Pan-religious (Roman Catholic and Buddhist influences): To drop the illusion that you are separate from All That Is and Ever Has Been.

Church of Jesus Christ of Latter-Day Saints: I speak to God daily. I pray individually both morning and evening, as a family in the evening before bed, and at all meals. I also pray in my heart at moments throughout any given day and speak to God when I need help or advice or just want to tell Him something. I believe He is always present and listening to our prayers and answers them through the Holy Ghost, impressions, and even in some cases audible voice, or the appearance of angels or God Himself. Just as with any relationship, the more time you spend with another person, the more you get to know them. As I draw my heart closer to God through prayer, study, and reflection, the more easily I feel His presence and recognize His answers to my prayers.

Non-denominational Universalist: All of us speak to God when we pray and thank Him for all that He has given and ask for what we need. How God speaks/communicates with you cannot be explained/understood within the physical limitations of human mind with which this question has been framed.

Sikh on paths of Sikhi: Yes, yes, learning to listen and be aware.

Jewish (Traditional/Orthodox): Not answerable in a brief survey.

Jewish (Ultraorthodox / Chabad Lubavitch): Yes when I pray. He speaks to me through His Torah. I become aware of G-d by obeying His will.

14.   How does your religion define good, and is it necessary for a person to be an adherent of your religion to be good?

Shia Muslim (Twelver): It comes back to the heart and one's purity of mind, intention and their actions. The topic of "good" is a massive philosophical discussion I can't sum up in few words. No, one does not have to be a Muslim to be good.

Evangelical Christian: Good is defined by acting and reacting in just, moral ways. It consists in being other-centered and seeking the good of another. All people are capable of goodness regardless of their religion. We believe that God has revealed himself to all humanity in what we call natural revelation (the natural order of things, creation, the symmetry and organization of the cosmos, etc.).

Shinto: There is no good or bad. However we can pick up kegare (pollution) from every day such as cities, arguments, death, and negative people. If we do not cleanse this away it can make us ill physically and mentally.

Baptist: No one is capable of good apart from Jesus, but one need not be Baptist to know Jesus.

Orthodox Zoroastrian: "Doing good to others is not a duty. It is a joy, for it increases your own health and happiness." Zartošt.

Quaker: It's not necessary to be an adherent of the religion to be good. Good is defined by inward reflection and external actions that bring to bear the teachings of equality, peace, integrity, and simplicity.

Jewish: Good is defined as following the divine will as explained in the Torah. It is not necessary for a person to be an adherent of Judaism to be good since we believe the Torah obligates non-Jews only to observe the Seven Commandments given to Noah. We are good to the extent that we do what God wants. For Jews, that is following the 613 Commandments of the Written and Oral Torah. For non-Jews, it is following the Seven Commandments given to Noah.

Taoist when pressed: There's no such "thing" as good or bad.

Sunni Muslim (Qadiri Sufi): Obeying God's commandments, people of my religion should strive to be good and emulate the Prophet, because his Sunnah, or tradition, is the path to success and righteousness.

Anglican: Goodness is defined by God's character. So as far as we act like God and do the things He does we are doing good. We are commanded to do good because God has been good to us. A person who does not do good could not have understood God's goodness.

Sikh: Emphasis is on good Karma: honest living, hard work helping others, daily prayer instead of empty rituals.

Jewish (Agnostic Secular): It is not necessary to be an adherent of Judaism to be good. Non-Jews have seven laws which they must keep, though Jews have 613. Good is to keep the laws and follow God's will. Agnosticism is not codified and does not define.

Episcopalian; Anglo-Catholic: Good is described as love toward others, and love toward God (which includes love toward God's creation). There are many ways to achieve this but no human is capable of being perfectly good until the reinstatement of the heavenly kingdom and the final redemption from sin. It is not necessary to adhere to a specific religion to achieve this.

Pentecostal/Calvinist: The traditionalist western view of good, yes or at least have repented.

Taoist: Don't f*%k with other people – leave them be; so I'd say it is necessary to be good.

No religion, just the Tao: There is a parable "One day, the horse escaped into the hills and when the farmer's neighbors sympathized with the old man over his bad luck, the farmer replied, "Bad luck? Good luck? Who knows?" A week later, the horse returned with a herd of wild horses from the hills, and the neighbors congratulated the farmer on his good luck. He replied,

"Good luck? Bad luck? Who knows?" Then, when the farmer's son was attempting to tame one of the wild horses he fell off its back and broke his leg. Everyone again sympathized with the farmer over his bad luck. But the farmer's reaction was, "Bad luck? Good luck? Who knows?" Some weeks later, the army marched into the village and drafted every able-bodied youth they found. When they saw the farmer's son with his broken leg, they let him stay." Good? Bad? Who knows?

Multi-Religious: Deity is good. Humans can't be good, but they can approach goodness through submission to deity. Goodness isn't an individual parameter. Either all humans are approaching goodness or none are. If all humans submitted to any legitimate (revealed) deity all would approach goodness.

Christian: To love and serve fellow man, and love and serve God. And no – all can be good.

Sunni Muslim: They are good if they adhere to the principles.

Quaker (follower of George Fox): There are none good but those who follow the voice of Christ, the Word of God. He is the source of all goodness.

Anglican: We can do nothing good without Christ. The Good is becoming holy and cultivating virtue.

Catholic: Good is anything that comes from God. A person doesn't need to be a Catholic to be good.

Born Again Christian: God is perfect, holy, just, righteous, pure, without darkness, cannot lie, no shadow of turning, gives not the spirit of fear, is not the author of confusion – pure goodness with removal of self, reason for being good is because of your love of Christ. Self-sacrificing good for the purpose of no other reason but for the Lord isn't possible outside of God's Faith. Unbelieving People can be good, but there's always a reason behind it and it's never Christ

Anglo-Catholic: To both allow individuals to have freedoms unless it would directly hurt someone else, yet also care for the people who need help.

Christian: God is good, and no.

Buddhist: Being compassionate toward all life is important in Buddhism and is exemplified by the Buddha's teachings of the Noble Eightfold Path. In Zen good and bad are merely concepts that one can get entangled in. Becoming aware of the Buddha nature and expressing it in daily life leads naturally to being good to others, without trying.

Bahá'í: All of what God creates is good, and evil is simply the absence of that good. Although anyone can do good deeds, or believe in the correct teachings and love God, to do both is what Baha'u'llah asks. He says neither belief nor action is acceptable without the other. This means anyone can do good action to others, but that person's intention for doing it matters to their own individual development. And vice versa for those who have good intention and do not translate it into action.

Atheist: Being empathetic to other people, not bringing harm to another person with our actions, and giving other people the same respect we expect until they've disrespected us.

Christian – Anglican: Good is acting in a way that brings you closer to God. Anglicans can be torn on this issue but generally most would say that those outside of Christianity can still be a good person, even if they do not have the truth.

Christian – Anglican: That's an incredibly broad question. Love your neighbor as yourself. Obviously anyone "should be" capable of this.

Agnostic: N/A.

Eliminative Materialist: Definitions of good are self-stable states, like natural selection. Value pluralism. We don't believe there's a single definition of good, but that there are multiple equally objectively correct answers. We do believe there are some things that cannot be moral though, like an infinite progression, or immortality. Other people can certainly be moral regardless of whether they follow our religion or not.

Chinese Buddhist with Taoist Leanings: Good is irrelevant. Virtue springs from being at one with life, not virtue for the sake of virtue.

I don't have a religion: I don't have a religion but secular humanism is about treating everyone like you want to be treated.

Taoist: To oversimplify, Taoism specifically points out that 'good' and 'bad' are overly simplistic.

Religious Society of Friends (Quaker): Jesus informs the rich, young ruler who seeks eternal life that there is "none good but one, that is, God" (Mark 10:18). Friends (originally) were in unity with the spirit of Christ, and would have concurred. Today, however, certain ideals and values among Liberals are the standards of goodness.

Agnostic Buddhist: Good is defined by what is the right thing to do. As I have said I do not know how others are able to lie to themselves and continue to believe it. I know when I try to lie to myself. I know it is false. No matter what I tell myself, I always know what is the right thing to do, deep down. I feel as though listening to the "good" is best. I also know it is sometimes difficult. Circumstance can change the black and white to many different shades of grey. It is best to try, knowing that you might not always succeed.

Quaker (Christian): No one has to be one of us to be good. To be good you must: do no harm, love unconditionally, and be a positive voice in your community.

Taoist: It does not and no.

Jewish, mainly Reform: According to commandments and mitzvot, good deeds.

Daoist: Non-doing is good, forced action and doing things one does not actually enjoy or need is bad. It would be difficult to call oneself a Daoist without following Daoist ethics.

Daoist: What is "good"? Knowing that is part of becoming wise.

Open ended, minded: We cannot define good or bad. For we cannot know the future of any action even if we think it may be good now, it may bring misfortune later on.

Eastern Orthodox: Good is that which God has created, as He Himself declares all things to be good in the first chapter of Genesis (and the word used in Greek, kalos, also means "beautiful"). All things are good by nature, even the demons, and so one does not need to be an Orthodox Christian to be good by nature, and created to fulfill this goodness. However, with the fall of Adam and Eve, we are found unable to fulfill this objective of goodness, except with the grace of God. There are two types of grace: calling grace is the grace present outside of the Church, which calls all people of all nations to join the Church, and saving grace is the grace within the Church, which restores the defigured image of God inside of us so that we may become truly in the image of God again and attain theosis (deification, that is, to become Christ-like, or to become by grace what God is by nature). If someone outside of the Church is saved, it is in spite of their sins and blasphemies and thanks to the prayers of Orthodox Christians – the normal path to salvation is only the Orthodox Church, apart from which there is no salvation.

Eastern Orthodox: Evil is the lack of good. Evil is the twisting of something that was meant to be good. It is necessary to be "good".

Spiritual: Good is providing a need for someone else.

Eastern Orthodox: Good is subjective, but no, all sinners are called.

Daoist: Good is what you know to be good innately. Being good is just having empathy. It is not necessary to be good to know what good is.

Undefined: Adherence is not only not mandatory, but not encouraged. Goodness is goodness no matter what religion.

Taoist: I don't think that Taoism concerns very much about what is good.

Sunni Muslim: Good is defined by not harming others. Non-believers can indeed be good.

Buddhist with a splash of Christianity, Taoism and Raja Yoga: Goodness would be in line with acting in ways that decrease suffering and increase skillful qualities such as calmness, mindfulness and generosity. By acting in this way you reduce the suffering you cause to yourself and others. It is not! Anyone can be good.

Muslim: "Righteousness is [in] one who believes in Allah, the Last Day, the angels, the Book, and the prophets and gives wealth, in spite of love for it, to relatives, orphans, the needy, the traveler, those who ask [for help], and for freeing slaves; [and who] establishes prayer and gives zakah; [those who] fulfill their promise when they promise; and [those who] are patient in poverty and hardship and during battle. Those are the ones who have been true, and it is those who are the righteous."

Buddhist: All actions (karma) produce results in kind. Unwholesome actions bring undesirable results; wholesome actions bring desirable results.

Pan-religious (Roman Catholic and Buddhist influences): I do not believe in a good-bad duality, and hold no beliefs, so I cannot define 'good' and cannot tie it to adhering to a set of beliefs.

Church of Jesus Christ of Latter-Day Saints: We believe that there is one truth – that things can be good or bad. There are many things that can be good that are not necessarily of religious significance. However, in the religious context, following God's commandments and Christ's example for us is how we choose the right and live a "good" life. It is not necessary for a person to be a member of the Church to be a good person. However, membership in the Church and making and keeping sacred covenants with God is necessary to achieve exaltation.

Non-denominational Universalist: All that does not harm others by word, deed or action is good and to be in such a state of mind bondage with any religion is not necessary.

Sikh on paths of Sikhi: We define good as Divine virtues. For example, speaking and acting in truth is a Divine virtue. Lying and cheating is not. The goal is to bring out the Divinity within you, which means behaving in a Divine-like manner. These are broadly laid out in a section of the Guru Granth Sahib called the Mool Mantar: Equality, Truth, Creative and existing Without Fear, Without Enemies. No, one doesn't need to adhere to Sikhi alone to be good.

Jewish (Traditional/Orthodox): Good people exist in all religious traditions. Our tradition defines goodness and decency in terms of the seven Noahide laws.

Jewish (Ultraorthodox / Chabad Lubavitch): Good is whatever G-d commands. At Sinai He gave a system of beliefs and practices for all mankind

Peter Brown

15. What does your religion say about the soul?

Shia Muslim (Twelver): It is created but does not die after the body dies.

Evangelical Christian: Every person is created with a soul that is differentiated from the physical nature of the person. The soul alone is eternal. It indwells a preborn fetus.

Shinto: There are many aspects of the soul in Shinto – too many to comment here.

Baptist: It was breathed out of God and into humanity and is immortal.

Orthodox Zoroastrian: Mainyus are the non-physical forms of us kept in our body until death which are released unto heaven for eternal peace of the wise Lord.

Quaker: A great deal. Soul is one's divine connection to God. Inner Light. Consciousness. I don't know. It's important, because we've all got one, and we've all got the proclivity to better it.

Jewish: The soul, unlike the body, is eternal and non-physical. In life, it is confined to the physical body. After the death of the body, the soul lives on experiencing the bliss of the divine presence to the extent that one followed the divine will during one's physical existence.

Taoist when pressed: Nothing.

Sunni Muslim (Qadiri Sufi): It comes from God and is our most elementary and basic form, yet the most versatile form we have.

Anglican: Humans are taught to be body and soul.

Sikh: The soul is immortal, it can be reborn and be reincarnated in any other form. Death is not the end for the soul; in fact the body is an article of clothing which can be discarded any time.

Jewish (Agnostic Secular): Agnosticism is not codified. Judaism, as I said, has conflicting and sometimes complicated beliefs, which I haven't delved into much.

Episcopalian; Anglo-Catholic: The soul is a part of each person and carries the light of God within it. I'm not sure what else it specifically states.

Pentecostal/Calvinist: It is corrupt.

Taoist: Not sure.

No religion, just the Tao: Not much.

Multi-Religious: Several revealed scriptures describe the soul. Believe from them whatever you can.

Christian: The early church was not so Descartian [Cartesian] as we are today so it is hard to tell. There is a sense we will be resurrected, however.

Quaker (follower of George Fox): There is that in man that is of the Earth: "And God formed man out of the dust of the Earth..." There is also that in man that has its origin in God: "And God breathed into man the breath of life and man became a living being..." The soul of man has no rest until man comes again to hear and obey the voice of the Creator.

Anglican: That it is immortal.

Catholic: That's a vague question. Not sure what to say besides we all have one.

Born Again Christian: It's eternal, the real you, and it will live forever in either heaven or hell.

Anglo-Catholic: The essence of a person.

Christian: It's very ambiguous.

Buddhist: There is no single, independent soul. There is only awareness, Nirvana, the Buddha nature.

Bahá'í: Explained a bit earlier. A "sign of God", "emanated" from Him but not a piece of Him, wholly spiritual and not part of the body, intimately connected to intellect and our rational/reasoning skills. Often referred to as the rational soul.

Atheist: That it doesn't exist.

Christian – Anglican: It was created by God and is eternal. It will reunite with the physical body during the resurrection and will reside with God forever.

Christian – Anglican: It is the part of the human that never dies.

Agnostic: On the fence.

Eliminative Materialist: As with God: we believe the concept of a soul relies on faulty premises.

Chinese Buddhist with Taoist Leanings: When you have a thought, are you the thinker of the thought or the one listening to the thought?

I don't have a religion: There is no soul.

Taoist: "Nothing" or "everything" depending on who you ask! "Soul" seems to me like a concept from other religions, rather than a real thing. If you mean 'consciousness' and life-after-death and so forth, the answer is that life is clearly continuous between you and me and reality (otherwise I wouldn't be writing this, and you wouldn't be reading it). The idea that it 'arrived' or can be 'taken away' is just fear talking. The Tao Te Ching doesn't say this, but it taught me a way of thinking and this is the conclusion I've come to.

Religious Society of Friends (Quaker): Quakers believe that the soul is given by God.

Agnostic Buddhist: The soul is a being in another dimension, of sorts. To me, once the body dies, the soul can manifest on the other plane and further its quest. I do not believe this is the only place to learn. The rules will be a bit different there, so I cannot answer anything more about that. This is what I choose to believe.

Quaker (Christian): The soul is your true life. It is where the light of God shines.

Taoist: Like death, many things. Again, the understanding of "religion" must be expanded beyond Judeo-Christian concepts.

Jewish, mainly Reform: I'm not sure.

Daoist: The human is formed from the interaction of heaven and earth, and there are three heavenly spirits and seven earthly spirits in the body. Thus it can be said that it is an illusion to think of a human as a unified individual.

Daoist: What's a "soul"?

Open ended, minded: We are not sure. Is it spirit? Is it a feeling? Is it the source of our mind? We do not know.

Eastern Orthodox: The body is our corporal flesh, the soul is our center of consciousness and personality and "self", and the spirit is the breath of life that animates and connects both. Death is an unnatural aberration that separates the soul from the body, but at the second coming of Jesus (the eschaton) all souls will be reunited with their body.

Eastern Orthodox: Everybody has one. It was corrupted by the flesh during the fall, and our savior has come to restore the ability to reunite ourselves with God's will (Theosis).

Spiritual: It exists in all of us. However do not confuse it with consciousness.

Eastern Orthodox: It says too much to put here.

Daoist: Ripples in a pond.

Undefined: Anything that moves to a rhythm, has a soul.

Taoist: Not much, I think.

Sunni Muslim: After death the only thing that remains is the soul.

Buddhist with a splash of Christianity, Taoism and Raja Yoga: That asking questions like this is a waste of time.

Muslim: Humans have been given a very limited knowledge about it.

Buddhist: The Buddhist doctrine of anatta or not-self is that there is no enduring self, soul or inner-agency at the center of experience. This doctrine is unique to Buddhism.

Pan-religious (Roman Catholic and Buddhist influences): That it is an illusion.

Church of Jesus Christ of Latter-Day Saints: We believe that our souls are the spiritual manifestation of our bodies, they have genders and identities just like we do in our physical presence. We are made in the image of God. Our soul is immutable. Our traits and characteristics are tied to our soul and our desires and personalities will be the same after this life as they are here on earth.

Non-denominational Universalist: Thread of life is separate from body and mind. You can understand this from the following illustration. • What belongs to you is NOT YOU; • Your car belongs to you but it is not YOU

• Your house belongs to you but it is not YOU • Your son, wife and relatives belong to you but none of them is YOU • Your leg, arm, head and other parts of the body belong to you but are not YOU. • Your whole body and mind belong to you but both these are not YOU. What really are YOU? Can you tell others? If you have an answer to this question, you will understand what is called SOUL in your body because that SOUL is yours.

Sikh on paths of Sikhi: The soul is the Divine Force that I have been referring to in previous answers.

Jewish (Traditional/Orthodox): The soul exists; it is a unique gift from God, given only to humans. Jews uphold the idea of "human exceptionalism."

Jewish (Ultraorthodox / Chabad Lubavitch): It is more real than the body. It is a part of G-d.

Peter Brown

16. What does your religion prescribe in terms of behavior toward others, and what is the source of that prescription?

Shia Muslim (Twelver): As in Mazdaism [Zoroastrianism], "Good words, good thoughts, good deeds;" their maxim is at the heart of Islam (as they're part of our prophetic lineage).

Evangelical Christian: Scripture guides our behavior toward others. The Golden Rule is what we are called to observe. We are also called to share our experience of God with others.

Shinto: Treat others with respect, we are representations of the Kami, children of the Kami and we must keep ourselves on the correct path.

Baptist: "Do to others as you would have them do to you." The fundamental baseline of this is the concept that all people are created in the image and likeness of God; therefore, all people (even ones we disagree with) are worthy of respect and kindness.

Orthodox Zoroastrian: I believe the biggest goal of Zoroastrianism is teaching that good manners is always the key and answer you are looking for. Thus the iconic Humata Hukhta Huvarshta (Good thought Good words Good deeds) it's like, the flowing blood of Zoroastrianism in its veins. It's similar to Christianity's law of love.

Quaker: Be respectful towards others. No killing, ever. Racism, sexism, really any "ism" is bad because we're all divine and equal. The source is the inner light in all.

Jewish: The great Rabbi Hillel, who lived about 2100 years ago, said that the essence of the entire Torah can be summarized as "That which is hateful to you, do not do to your fellow." The rest of the Torah, Rabbi Hillel said, is explanation. He then advised the person to whom he was speaking to learn it. The source of the prescription on behavior toward others is the Torah, which contains numerous commandments concerning how to treat one's fellow. Those Commandments are summarized in the second half of the Ten Commandments proscribing murder, adultery, kidnapping, perjury, and envy. Each of those is merely a subject heading on numerous derivative proscriptions, including physical violence (unless in self-defense), stealing, gossiping, and much more.

Taoist when pressed: See the answer under question 8.

Sunni Muslim (Qadiri Sufi): We must be merciful to the creation and we must not cause harm to others. Abu Sirmah reported: The Messenger of Allah, peace and blessings be upon Him, said, "Whoever harms others, then Allah will harm him. Whoever is harsh with others, then Allah will be harsh with him." Source: Sunan al-Tirmidhī 1940.

Anglican: Love your neighbors as you love yourself. Demonstrated by God's love for us by sending Jesus to die on our behalf.

Sikh: Kindness, empathy and compassion. Equality for all irrespective of caste, color or creed. The teachings in the Guru Granth Sahib is the main prescription.

Jewish (Agnostic Secular): Torah says "You shall not take vengeance or bear a grudge against your kinsfolk. Love your neighbor as yourself". Rabbi Hillel the Elder said: "That which is hateful to you, do not do to your fellow. That is the whole Torah; the rest is the explanation; go and learn". Also the 10 Commandments from the Torah and many other laws and the seven laws of Gentiles which include some interpersonal relations laws and which are for Jews and gentiles alike. Agnostic as before.

Episcopalian; Anglo-Catholic: It says to love others as yourself, as representations of God in the world. This primarily comes from scriptural commandments but is emphasized by historical church teaching.

Pentecostal/Calvinist: Treat others the way you want to be treated.

Taoist: Let them be them.

No religion, just the Tao: The Tao does not have any rules in this regard, it leaves it up to the Tao in you.

Multi-Religious: Several scriptures prescribe regulations. Follow of them whatever you feel is just.

Christian: Love others as Christ loved us.

Sunni Muslim: Treat others with care.

Quaker (follower of George Fox): Jesus told his followers "do unto others as you would have them do unto you." But how are we to fulfill that admonition? Micah admonished that we are to love mercy, do justice, and walk humbly with God. All these admonitions are useless if we do not humbly follow the voice of God. For the power to live righteously is received when we step out in obedience to the voice of God.

Anglican: Love (Agape) that is commanded by God.

Catholic: Treat others with love and as well as you possibly can. The source of that prescription is a mixture of common sense, Scripture, Sacred Tradition and natural law.

Born Again Christian: Mark 12:30 and thou shalt love the Lord thy God with all thy heart, and with all thy soul, and with all thy mind, and with all thy strength: this is the first commandment. 12:31 and the second is like, namely this, Thou shalt love thy neighbor as thyself. There is no other commandment greater than these.

Anglo-Catholic: Act as Jesus did in the Bible, love without bias.

Christian: Love each other, directly from God.

Buddhist: The Buddha prescribed the Noble Eightfold Path. Each part of the path is dependent on all the other parts of the path in order to both attain enlightenment and be good to others. One can't just isolate and practice a single part of the path without practicing the others.

Bahá'í: Individuals must love and support all others. Communities must love, support, and create environments where education, friendship, advancement can occur. Institutions must administer judgement (only they can judge), guide all, and be loving and supportive as well.

Atheist: It has no source but collectively we try to be respectful. That can be difficult, however, when everyone else believes that our lack of belief alone automatically makes us awful people.

Christian – Anglican: "Thou shalt love the Lord thy God with all thy heart, and with all thy soul, and with all thy mind. This is the first and great commandment. And the second is like unto it, Thou shalt love thy neighbour as thyself. On these two commandments hang all the law and the prophets." - Jesus

Christian – Anglican: Scripture, reason, and tradition.

Agnostic: N/A

Eliminative Materialist: The most ethical course is non-interaction. Take a different niche and avoid interfering with others.

Chinese Buddhist with Taoist Leanings: Eightfold Path but as mentioned previously virtue is an extension of a clear mind.

I don't have a religion: Treat everyone equally. This is basic empathy but without it the secular laws are based on the same basic principles.

Taoist: Taoism is often vague, but it's quite specific on this point! It teaches you to pass on knowledge of the Tao, or, less recursively, encourages you to help people find their own way – help them not to see things as good or bad – the value of non-action in a situation where you're compelled to act. I'm oversimplifying, but that's a summary of my understanding.

Religious Society of Friends (Quaker): A hearing, obedient response to God's will known inwardly is Friends standard for behavior toward others, and in all other areas. Jesus's prescription in Matthew 7:12 would be heeded, as well: "Whatsoever ye would that men should do to you, do ye even so to them: for this is the law and the prophets."

Agnostic Buddhist: Compassion. The source is through understanding. The more you try to understand another person and who they are the more compassion can develop.

Quaker (Christian): Jesus commands us to love others as we would ourselves. We must always strive to be compassionate towards others. Wish them no harm and do them no harm. Aid them when they need aid. Love them without qualification. If they have done evil, pray for them and engage them in the spirit of reconciliation.

Taoist: Be compassionate, be frugal, dare to not be first before others.

Jewish, mainly Reform: Pretty much the Golden rule. Lots of old law regarding people and property.

Daoist: Non-doing, and acting to others according to one's spontaneous kindness. To be like water, which sinks to the dirtiest and darkest places to secretly nurture others without intentionally trying.

Daoist: You have to figure that out for yourself.

Open ended, minded: One's behavior depends on the context of their life. There is no one path to enlightenment.

Eastern Orthodox: We must do toward others as we wish they would toward us, but more precisely, we must act toward others as we would toward Jesus – because He is truly and mystically present in them, as they carry His image. The commandment to do toward others as we wish they would toward us is found in the things God has revealed to Moses, but Christ repeats them again with clarity during His mission, and this holy doctrine has been kept by the apostles and their successors, the bishops.

Eastern Orthodox: Love one another, always want what's best for others (their salvation).

Spiritual: Golden Rule.

Eastern Orthodox: The Golden Rule.

Daoist: Act in accord with your nature. If people do this, most will act well, because most are good.

Undefined: The Golden Rule but instead treat others as the best version of yourself would like to be treated.

Taoist: It basically says to not be a jerk. I think that it does teach a certain degree of humility.

Sunni Muslim: Throughout the Quran and the Hadiths you are told to treat others with respect and sincerity.

Buddhist with a splash of Christianity, Taoism and Raja Yoga: Kindness, generosity, honesty etc. Showing others kindness is conducive for our own minds on the path; it also makes it easier for others to find happiness.

Muslim: Indeed, Allah orders justice and good conduct and giving to relatives and forbids immorality and bad conduct and rebellion. He admonishes you that perhaps you will be reminded. 16:90.

Buddhist: Compassion and benevolence. There's that whole karma thing.

Pan-religious (Roman Catholic and Buddhist influences): To understand that one is not separate from others; the boundaries between one and another is an illusion. So when you harm another, you harm yourself.

Church of Jesus Christ of Latter-Day Saints: We are the Church of Jesus Christ and we believe that He leads our Church. He is our exemplar and we are to emulate Him in how we live our lives. We are to show love to others. We use the terms "Brother" and "Sister" to refer to each other and believe that we are all children of God.

Through this regular reminder we hope to keep our hearts softened to others and engage ourselves in service to our families, our community, and the world.

Non-denominational Universalist: Treat all human beings equally irrespective of their religious beliefs, color, race or nationality, devote one/tenth of your time and resources towards voluntary services that make a marked difference in the lives of others and wish peace and happiness in the lives of all. Source of these virtues spring from innumerable versus recorded in the Holy Guru Granth Sahib by our Gurus and other Holy Saints hailing from different religious beliefs and faiths.

Sikh on paths of Sikhi: Help those in need, earn an honest living, ensure equity amongst all, build trust and strength with your community, always remember the Divine and behave with the virtues of the Divine in all you do. All guidance is from Guru Granth Sahib.

Jewish (Traditional/Orthodox): Sixty three tractates of Talmud exist to answer that question, as well as literally thousands of volumes of Rabbinic discourse. Rabbi Hillel's formulation (which preceded the New Testament's "Golden Rule") works as well as it did 2,000 years ago: "What is hateful to you, do not do to others. All the rest is commentary. I suggest you study the commentary."

Jewish (Ultraorthodox / Chabad Lubavitch): Love your fellow as yourself.

Peter Brown

17. What can people do to improve themselves?

Shia Muslim (Twelver): Seek deeply within, first psychologically, then spiritually. I don't see religion as a form of "self-improvement," though, if that's what this implies.

Evangelical Christian: We never are capable of achieving God's standard of righteousness. We need a Savior who credits our moral account with his moral reserve. We do not follow God and keep his commandments to approve ourselves unto God. Rather, we study and worship and pray to get to know our Creator better. We deny ourselves in acts of service as a way of expressing our gratitude to God.

Shinto: Pray every day to the Kami, respect ancestors and elders, spend time in nature, perform misogi (cleansing).

Baptist: Study God's word and come to know His son Jesus personally.

Orthodox Zoroastrian: Always think. And think a lot before doing or saying something. And always choose the nik (kind) path and avoid hurting others.

Quaker: Improve your actions towards others.

Jewish: Spiritually, the best way to improve oneself is to study and observe the Torah. Ethically, one must work on developing good character traits (e.g. peacefulness, love for one's fellow, mercy, humility, truth-telling, joy, and modesty) and proper behaviors (e.g. acting kindly to one's fellow and even to animals, being respectful to parents and elders, being hospitable to guests, and giving charity). One should also take care of one's health and endeavor to keep one's body healthy through exercise. Intellectually, one can improve oneself through the study of both Torah and non-Torah knowledge. Maintaining healthy relationships is also critical.

Taoist when pressed: "Know thyself", is the same as knowing "Oneness", is the same as being the best person you can be.

Sunni Muslim (Qadiri Sufi): In my religion we follow the Sufi path and self-improvement is a goal of ours. There are many methods that each order professes in.

Anglican: Depends what they mean. Improvement that actually matters can only come through trusting God and obeying him.

Sikh: Be attuned of their feelings and surroundings, support for emotional and physical needs. You can only help others if you take care of yourself first

Jewish (Agnostic Secular): Think about their actions and adjust them to follow "That which you hate do not do to your fellow"

Episcopalian; Anglo-Catholic: Seek a greater connection with God and with others; use kindness as a lesson in love and compassion; acknowledge mistakes and make tangible steps to rectify them when possible. People should develop the disciplines of forgiveness, patience, humility, selflessness, and empathy in order to better care for themselves and for others, including all of God's creation.

Pentecostal/Calvinist: Meditate God's word, strive to become better.

Taoist: Abide.

No religion, just the Tao: Nothing.

Multi-Religious: Self-improvement is an egocentric practice which came from the non-theistic field of psychology. Humans can approach goodness by submitting to deity.

Christian: Find a church; read and contemplate; develop a spiritual discipline.

Quaker (follower of George Fox): Wait in the light of Christ to be shown their true condition and how to come out of corruption into the life of Christ.

Anglican: Prayer, reading scripture sacraments and rejoicing in God's salvation.

Catholic: Well there's the natural path like make goals and try to keep them but that can't happen without grace. They can just ask Jesus for help, too.

Born Again Christian: 1 Corinthians 10:31. Whether therefore ye eat, or drink, or whatsoever ye do, do all to the glory of God.

Anglo-Catholic: Read, hike, cook, pray. Anything that enables self-reflection. To love others, first we have to love ourselves.

Christian: Seek God.

Buddhist: Meditate! Exercise. Drink a lot of water. Get away from civilization every once in a while and get out into the natural world. Become more like children, carefree, sincere, and playful. Be vulnerable with others. Stop being so attached to one's ego.

Bahá'í: Search for God themselves, free from prejudice. With or without that knowledge, serve others. Develop our spiritual qualities.

Atheist: Learn something new every day, strive to take care of ourselves and each other

Christian – Anglican: Focus on being a loving person to others and yourself. Seek a connection with God and act as He would want.

Christian – Anglican: They can't. Only God can improve us.

Agnostic: Help others, don't be selfish, figure out what's important in life, love.

Eliminative Materialist: Ritual, analyzing one's mind, meditation, learning skills and how the things they use are made, and becoming self-sufficient in the things they depend on.

Chinese Buddhist with Taoist Leanings: Mature into a being of inner peace.

I don't have a religion: Set a goal and achieve it.

Taoist: People can learn to separate themselves from their reactions, their language, and their disbelief in the intentions of others. If I say there is no such thing as a 'soul', yet the receiver of this sentence finds it ridiculous because they equate their soul with experiencing life, then they can choose to find that person either crazy, wrong, or they can realize it's a problem of language – and they can try to find another way to connect to the person about this point. If humanity can solve this one, we will be unrecognizably and beautifully new, as a species.

Religious Society of Friends (Quaker): People can improve themselves by loving the truth above all things, for this leads to an inward relationship with God.

Agnostic Buddhist: Honesty. Once you start being honest with yourself you can move forward in whatever direction.

Quaker (Christian): Improving yourself begins in the mind. Moving towards a calm state of mind will bear plentiful fruits in the world. Wholesome thought brings us closer to God.

Taoist: Make time to be silent.

Jewish, mainly Reform: Study. Be kind. Teach your children. Respect the earth.

Daoist: Stop trying to improve, but self-reflect and remove that which is unnecessary.

Daoist: They can practice a Kung Fu, or a diligent thoughtful practice aimed at becoming a better, more wise person.

Open ended, minded: Exercise and eat clean.

Eastern Orthodox: Repent of their sins.

Eastern Orthodox: Repent of our fallen state of flesh and strive to achieve a knowledge of God – Theosis.

Spiritual: Empathize.

Eastern Orthodox: Go to Divine Liturgy.

Daoist: Excellence is attained through discipline and practice.

Undefined: Listen to themselves. Don't take themselves too seriously.

Taoist: Pay attention to how everything flows around you. Then you'll know what to do and how to do it most easily.

Sunni Muslim: People should use good judgement and morals.

Buddhist with a splash of Christianity, Taoism and Raja Yoga: 1. The unexamined life is not worth living. 2. Meditate.

Muslim: Humans should try to balance their duties toward both God and other humans.

Buddhist: Study scripture, contemplate the teachings, work toward perfecting one's virtue.

Pan-religious (Roman Catholic and Buddhist influences): Nothing; people are perfect as they are.

Church of Jesus Christ of Latter-Day Saints: People can pray, seek guidance from the Lord, and from their Church leaders to work on behaviors they want to improve. Through constant work to improve ourselves and communion with God, we can build any skill, improve knowledge, soften our hearts, and gain a testimony of any aspect of the Gospel.

Non-denominational Universalist: People can improve themselves by accepting the fact that people are different and it is hard to change them as others resist change. Never stop learning new things and adding to your knowledge. Become an example of perfect human being and people will start automatically following you without the necessity of compelling them to change for their own good.

Sikh on paths of Sikhi: Tons of stuff! Depends what is not working out in the first place.

Jewish (Traditional/Orthodox): Study and follow God's law; draw closer to His will.

Jewish (Ultraorthodox / Chabad Lubavitch): Before doing or saying anything decide if this is appropriate or not.

Peter Brown

18. What exists, and where did it come from?

Shia Muslim (Twelver): The universe, which we are a part of, which emanated and manifested from the one central point (of God).

Evangelical Christian: All that is originated in the heart of God. All that is physical and spiritual came into existence from God's decision that it come to be.

Shinto: Kami came from the Abus, when the first Kami was born, the universe was born. We do not know why and we never will. It is beyond our comprehension.

Baptist: Everything God made exists, and it came from Him.

Orthodox Zoroastrian: I do not have knowledge of this and nor do I think anyone does.

Quaker: Who knows? We're all figuring that out together.

Jewish: I am tempted to answer with the first principle of Ayn Rand's philosophy of "objectivism" that "existence exists." But seriously, the only perfect existence is God, who did not come from anywhere but who is the Primary Cause of all other existence, including the physical universe and even spiritual existences such as angels and souls and thoughts. My baby book states that I asked my Mom at age six who made God. It is hard for an adult, let alone a six-year-old, to understand how God can have always existed without origin. My friend Rabbi S_____ once analogized the difference between the existence of God and the existence of anything else to the difference between the wetness of a cup of water and the wetness of a damp towel. The latter is merely conditionally wet. The former is wet in its very essence. Similarly, God's existence is essential, while all other existence is merely conditional (on the will of God).

Taoist when pressed: No thing, and so everything, and it came from a big-bang supposedly.

Sunni Muslim (Qadiri Sufi): God is the only true permanent existence, and everything has come from him. Everything other than God is temporary.

Anglican: Everything. God made it.

Sikh: The beginning and end of everything is God Almighty.

Jewish (Agnostic Secular): The physical world and universe, came from the Big Bang unless God fooled us. Maybe God, as I defined earlier, exists too. Maybe the Big Bang is God. Hard to comprehend the world and God not having a beginning yet as hard to comprehend them having a beginning.

Episcopalian; Anglo-Catholic: I don't know. We perceive our tangible world as well as intangible experiences such as dreams and memories but it is unclear that these exist or are simply part of our subjective perception.

Pentecostal/Calvinist: Everything that exists, it came from nothing and was created by God

Taoist: Huh?

No religion, just the Tao: Nothing does, but everything does, it didn't come from anything but at the same time it did.

Multi-Religious: All consciousness/awareness exists and it came from the first consciousness that is Deity.

Christian: God is the ground of being, so being is contingent on him. Our world and universe exist and perhaps many others.

Sunni Muslim: Allah and He was always there.

Quaker (follower of George Fox): I do not see the relevance of this question and do not have an answer.

Anglican: From God.

Catholic: This world exists, God exists. The question is kind of broad again but I understand it is intentionally so. The world was made by God.

Born Again Christian: All things came from God, He created it for His glory. He made all things, sin entered by Lucifer's pride tempting Adam and Eve – and God saved all things by His Son the Lord God Jesus Christ. It all came by the Word of God.

Anglo-Catholic: Not only what we see, and existence is without the restrictions of our perception. For example, the pyramids exist, but I've never seen them. Everything came from the Big Bang. As suns exploded elements were formed to create everything we see today. This is all according to God's plan.

Christian: The universe. I don't know.

Buddhist: There is only the Buddha Mind, and it has always been here.

Bahá'í: God is the Creator. A creator must have creation to be a creator, thus Baha'u'llah argues that God has always been, and always will be. Likewise creation has always been, and always will be, but has changed form from time to time. At the same time, God did create nature and the universe, and nature is His "will in this contingent world". It is a bit of a paradox, but also makes sense to me more than other explanations. As Baha'u'llah says, we cannot know God and His ways wholly.

Atheist: Anything with mass exists. To answer where everything came from would take far too long and require far too many sources of information.

Christian – Anglican: Everything. In the beginning God created it out of nothing.

Christian – Anglican: I have no idea.

Agnostic: Matter exists. It came from the Big Bang Theory as far as we know.

Eliminative Materialist: Existence is interaction, and an object is indistinguishable for the effects it has on the world. Things exist because it's an impossibility for nothing to exist, so the void outside the universe is a constant froth of new things springing into existence.

Chinese Buddhist with Taoist Leanings: Thus. Any guesses are heresy.

I don't have a religion: I don't know why anything exists but once anything exists everything is the complex arrangement of quantum fluctuations.

Taoist: Ha. That is the question. Taoism would say the 'it', whatever it is, came from the Tao. Which is actually different from the 'it' being the Tao. I exist, this keyboard exists, you exist, your screen exists, your book exists (and it sounds from these questions like it will be great) – that's as far as I can see in this moment.

Religious Society of Friends (Quaker): Creation exists and it came from God in the beginning.

Agnostic Buddhist: The only thing that really exist for certain is yourself. Even if it is all an illusion, you know for sure you exist. You can make changes. You can affect what you perceive around you. As far as I know, I have always been. I do not know where I came from, but from the moment of my earliest memory, I have always been here within myself. That's the only thing I am certain of.

Quaker (Christian): The world and the universe are of God's creation. God granted us a beautiful mind to reason with his creation. The "Big Bang" is simply the most beautiful thing of chance. Like the clockmaker, God set his creation up and let it run.

Taoist: The one, the two, the three, the ten thousand many things. These all exist, but so too does their perceived nullities.

Jewish, mainly Reform: There was darkness. And then light. And plants, animals, and man.

Daoist: I do not understand the question.

Daoist: The universe, and how would I know where it comes from?

Open ended, minded: We do not know.

Eastern Orthodox: What exists is "the heavens and earth, the visible and the invisible", as our creed says. Things in the realm of the observable and material, and things in the realm of the spiritual and immaterial, are what the cosmos consists of. All things come from nothing and were created by the Father, through the Son, in the Holy Spirit.

Eastern Orthodox: A Trinitarian Godhead, three distinct persons that are one essence, one God. It did not "come" from anywhere, it has always been, always will be. The logos (λόγοσ) was incarnate into human flesh for our sake to restore the ability to reunite with God.

Spiritual: Everything. Who cares?

Eastern Orthodox: All things were created by God.

Daoist: What is comes from what is not. Everything is defined by its limits.

Undefined: I exist in this moment right now, and don't need to know why.

Taoist: Everything seems to exist. It comes from the Big Bang, some 14 billion years ago.

Sunni Muslim: I cannot answer you where it came from, that's why it's a belief.

Buddhist with a splash of Christianity, Taoism and Raja Yoga: How could I possibly know this! (ha ha) Where were you before you were born?

Muslim: Allah, the Eternal Refuge. He neither begets nor is born, nor is there to Him any equivalent.

Buddhist: Buddhism doesn't have a creation myth. The beginning point is outside the range of possible.

Pan-religious (Roman Catholic and Buddhist influences): Nothing exists, and it came from nothing.

Church of Jesus Christ of Latter-Day Saints: Everything exists. We live in a reality that is governed by God and God's laws. I believe that everything we have is from God, including things like science. I believe God created the universe, and the earth upon which we live. Nothing comes from nothing. I believe God organized matter in something that could be similar to the "Big Bang." Just as surely as the physical world exists, so also is there a spiritual world that we are currently separated from, but which we will rejoin after our time on this earth.

Non-denominational Universalist: All existence is a manifestation of vibrations emanating from Almighty [universal source of Energy in the form of light and sound]. Remember that all forms of energy are invisible. You may recall that NASA studies have declared that all the planets, galaxies, stars etc. that we see in the Universe is only 4% of the total matter and 96% is still invisible/inexplicable. Therefore, origin of the matter is beyond the comprehension of human mind and intellect.

Sikh on paths of Sikhi: 'It' is self-existent and came from itself.

Jewish (Traditional/Orthodox): God exists, and always has. God didn't come from anywhere (sorry for those who think visiting aliens created life).

Jewish (Ultraorthodox / Chabad Lubavitch): The creation from   G-d.

19. What is the function of religious ritual, and how important is it in your religion?

Shia Muslim (Twelver): Highly important. Aside from the belief in the one, absolute, eternal God of absolute unity. Ritual is secondary and has to be authentic, or else it is empty actions. Experience before belief.

Evangelical Christian: Ritual is key. Traditions are vital. The rhythm of religious rites provide us with a balance. Ritual holds us together in an ever-changing world.

Shinto: Ritual is the center of Shinto. Its purpose is to speak with the Kami, make offerings, perform blessings, give thanks, and much more

Baptist: The purpose of meetings in a Baptist church is primarily twofold: (1) edification and teaching through the preaching of the word; (2) fellowship between believers.

Orthodox Zoroastrian: Not much really. They are just ceremonies that bear the goal of bringing the small group of us together.

Peter Brown

Quaker: Religious ritual is spurned. This is because God can be directly experienced by everybody.

Jewish: My religion does not really distinguish in principle between religious "ritual" and other obligations. I am not even sure what "ritual" means. Perhaps one way to define it is a religious observance that does not appear to have a rational meaning. If so, ritual is very important in Judaism since we understand God's Law to include both laws that our rational/understandable and those that cannot be humanly understood, at least not in entirety. Part of the way we show our absolute dedication to God is by observing even those commandments that have no rational explanation. One of the key principles of Judaism is "Naaseh v'neeshmah," meaning "We will do and we will hear (or understand)." The *doing* comes first. Then (and *only* then), we also do try to understand to our limited ability. More broadly, if ritual means communal prayer and traditional observances, they also serve to bind Jews to each other and to our ancestors.

Taoist when pressed: Useless.

Sunni Muslim (Qadiri Sufi): Prayer is prescribed five times a day and is one of the five pillars

Anglican: Not very. They have a tendency to become idols.

Sikh: For some it is a way of life and philosophy. It is very vital because lays a foundation for social justice, sharing, devotion and abolishment of superstitions and blind rituals which can be very detrimental to society.

Jewish (Agnostic Secular): In Judaism it is very important, as the whole religion is following laws, which are to be a light among the nations and unto the world and to follow God's will.

Episcopalian; Anglo-Catholic: Ritual is a means to discipline by providing a framework in which one may further develop one's own personal spirituality. Ritual is important to me and my religion as a way to connect with the broader history of the church and to provide continuity and familiarity as one explores the deep religious questions. Ritual serves to draw worship and religious action into the unconscious to make room for conscious relationships.

Pentecostal/Calvinist: Mainly community.

Taoist: Zip.

No religion, just the Tao: Zero function in basic Taoism; sects like saying that rituals can help you achieve immortality of some sort, though.

Multi-Religious: Revealed acts of worship are not the same as rituals. Rituals are made by humans for the purpose of approaching deity in an eclectic manner. Rituals are very important.

Christian: Two sacraments (for Episcopalians) and necessary.

Sunni Muslim: Religion is important but I should be more religious.

Quaker (follower of George Fox): The result of some 60 years of observation is that the function of religious ritual is to isolate oneself from hearing and following the voice of God.

Anglican: Yes.

Catholic: It helps put worshipers in the right mindset and it's the fitting thing. It can change slightly over time as long as the essential elements remain the same.

Born Again Christian: Rituals, religiosity, tradition are nothing but man's religious nature – they have no bearing on salvation, but are just a help to keep oneself in line and to aid in overcoming issues.

Anglo-Catholic: To praise and worship God. I think you could go to heaven without stepping into church, but I gain peace through the rituals. In other words, I find them important to myself, but they don't fit for everyone.

Christian: Connect us to God and each other, not hugely important.

Buddhist: Ritual seems very important to a lot of Zen practitioners because it instills discipline and mindfulness. For me it is not so important. Having a good laugh is much more Zen than doing laps around the Zendo.

Bahá'í: Dogma and blind repetition and imitation are forbidden and abolished by Baha'u'llah. There is ritual technically in the sense that Baha'is are told to pray daily and do other things a certain way...things that are repetitive and can become ritualistic. But outward rituals that have no deeper meaning or purpose (wearing certain clothing, doing certain actions, etc., particularly blindly) are forbidden. Baha'i communities have lots in common, but borrow customs from local culture for non-important aspects of community's life, and for those things Baha'u'llah did not prescribe or teach something. Dress, food, music, are not viewed as rituals and are up to the individual. Those actions that might be perceived as rituals, namely obligatory prayer, fasting, etc. are very important, but not due to their mildly ritualistic nature – rather their practical meaning and benefit.

Atheist: It's to put a person in that mindset. We don't have rituals.

Christian – Anglican: Rituals are a way for humans to feel the sacredness of prayer and is pleasing to God. God instituted ritual prayers first through the ancient Jewish peoples and again with the Apostles. When liturgy is torn down theology often goes with it.

Christian – Anglican: It centers our mind, actions, and hearts. It is the centerpiece of religion.

Agnostic: N/A.

Eliminative Materialist: Retraining the mind. We recognize that human actions are based on mental drives, but we also believe that emotion is only significant in the context it evolved in. Outside of that context (as in modern life) it's important to analyze what you desire and see if it still makes any sense in an objective context.

Chinese Buddhist with Taoist Leanings: Formal meditation is pretty good at rooting out the bullshit that I tell myself all day, and helping clear my mind.

I don't have a religion: I don't have a religion.

Taoist: This might be cynical, but I think most religious ritual is to keep a small set of habits alive that serve the spreading of the religion, with hopefully useful side-effects for the practitioners. In mine, you get out of it what you put into it. Personally I read a segment of the Tao Te Ching periodically, usually when I'm feeling anxious; it's very centering. Some have their own rituals, others none. Taoism prescribes no answer to this one, and relishes in the fact that it doesn't.

Religious Society of Friends (Quaker): Ritual plays no part in Friends faith because we seek to be guided by God who is the Spirit, which as the "wind bloweth where it listeth" (Jn. 3:8). Friends, who are born of the Spirit, follow this same Spirit.

Agnostic Buddhist: Meditation is important. Being able to silence your mind. The more often you do it the easier it becomes. Instead of sitting quietly to calm my mind, I now take moments in. I pause and absorb the moments that most take for granted. When I watch my daughter learning something new, I take that moment to appreciate everything about her. I memorize the look of determination, the process she uses ... the moment of accomplishment. I pause when I see something in nature that is exquisite, really. Like meditating on the Fibonacci sequence being present in everything. That is fun to think about, honestly. Really just taking in the small moments of internal appreciation epiphanies I find throughout. Then there are my rituals of forcing myself to see the good in the bad. It has brought me sadness at times but I prefer to find the good. It is a much more beautiful painting to memorize.

Quaker (Christian): We have very few rituals, they ultimately distract us from communion with God.

Taoist: Rituals serve to bring people into the right headspace to be more receptive for intuitive lessons.

Jewish, mainly Reform: Considered daily.

Daoist: Different types of rituals perform different functions; to bring one's actions closer to the Dao, to manipulate natural forces for the benefit of lay people, to petition spirits to assist in one's development and to aid the community, etc.

Daoist: It's a way of unifying a human culture both now and through time.

Open ended, minded: Depends on context, culture, language. To me? Very little.

Eastern Orthodox: Primarily, religious ritual is what surrounds the sacraments, or holy mysteries, which are the reality of the Gospel being made present to us here and now so that we may have communion with Jesus Christ. These mysteries are Baptism, Chrismation, Confession, Communion, Marriage, Ordination, and Holy Unction. Secondarily, ritual can be done in remembrance of the mission of Jesus on earth, and by extension of the lives of the apostles, of the Virgin Mary, of certain historical events in the Church...

Eastern Orthodox: It is very important. Our liturgics enhance our worship and help us to more perfectly, as possible, achieve Theosis.

Spiritual: To brainwash.

Eastern Orthodox: Worship. See also Jordan Peterson's response to why Orthodox Christians enjoy his rhetoric.

Daoist: Ritual brings order to chaos. If you want order then it's very important. If you don't want order then it's not very important.

Undefined: Reminders are always a good way to set me back on my present path.

Taoist: The only religious ritual that I constantly practice daily is qigong. Good for the body and the mind. It really relaxes and balances.

Sunni Muslim: It has some degree of importance, but there are exceptions. (Not obligatory for poor people to do Umrah etc.).

Buddhist with a splash of Christianity, Taoism and Raja Yoga: To cultivate skillful qualities of the mind. Very important, this is the core practice. Meditation facilitates every aspect of the path.

Muslim: Rituals are forms of worship. These symbolize our relation to God. For example, prayer symbolizes our unconditional obedience to God.

Buddhist: Buddhists are not attached to rites and ritual. The few we have are to help us get centered on the path.

Pan-religious (Roman Catholic and Buddhist influences): Ritual and theatre are the ways we speak to unconscious metaphysical realm, and arrive at the place beyond words.

Church of Jesus Christ of Latter-Day Saints: Our religion, like most others, has religious rituals. These rituals are with regard to the sacred covenants which we make with God at certain significant stages in our lives. Being able to repeat these covenants regularly allows us to remember the promises we made to the Lord and the promises the Lord made to us. Through the repetition we can recommit ourselves to keep our covenants and live a righteous life, following God's example.

Non-denominational Universalist: Religious rituals play an important part in the lives of those who are emotionally devotional. These do not appeal to those who measure them by way of logic and reasoning. Some rituals were initially instituted in some sects which sought to do good to mankind. However, over a period of time their original essence has been lost and those who observe them do so only by way of mental indulgence in religious rituals. Rituals have no importance in Sikh religion.

Sikh on paths of Sikhi: Rituals are helpful if they are meaningful. They can serve the function of bringing community together, or feeling the presence of the

Divine, or creating discipline and routine to live a happier life. Rather than ritual, in Sikhi there is the lifestyle of waking early and reflecting/meditating on the Divine as described in Guru Granth Sahib. This more than anything is the one ritual that guides how you behave.

Jewish (Traditional/Orthodox): Religious ritual uplifts and defines our days and years.

Jewish (Ultraorthodox / Chabad Lubavitch): They are divine commandments and are essential.

20. What else would you like to tell me?

Shia Muslim (Twelver): Baraka Allahu fika [may Allah bless you].

Evangelical Christian: I have enjoyed participating in your survey. I look forward to having the opportunity to read your results.

Baptist: Most Baptists are just folks who want to be left alone to worship how they see fit, try to live good Christ-centered lives, and be living examples of what Jesus can do to change our lives if we accept him.

Quaker: I don't think you can survey monkey someone's spirituality. You kinda have to talk to them in person about this stuff.

Jewish: Jews are known for responding to questions with questions. Though Friedrich Nietzsche was declared the official Nazi philosopher decades after his death, he was in fact a philo-semite, so maybe it is not surprising that he began his seminal work Beyond Good and Evil with "ein Stelldichein . . . von Fragen und Fragezeichen," a "rendezvous . . . of questions and question marks." Anyway, I'll answer this question with two questions: 1) Why do surveys always end with this question? There is always much else I can tell you, but it depends on what you want to know, which was articulated in Questions 1 through 20. If you want more, ask another specific question. 2) Hence, my second question: What else would you like to know?

Taoist when pressed: Sorry to be so vague, I'm not trying to come across as some kind of mystic or something, but life is very simple and it's only when we start asking questions that it gets complicated - not because it IS complicated, but because we need to break it into manageable bits and complex systems. Doing so is great for building space rockets, but cannot be applied to life, living, and understanding the reality of existence – which is what most religions are trying to do.

Sikh: Sikhism is one of the newest religions, originated 550 years ago. Embraces people from all paths of life, treats every one with equality, always helping through seva and langars and not afraid to speak up for the rights of others. Blessed to be born in this faith.

Episcopalian; Anglo-Catholic: I hope I was able to adequately answer the questions – I don't consider myself a theologian or expert by any means.

Pentecostal/Calvinist: Thanks!

No religion, just the Tao: I like you. Good luck with your book/paper, if you can please send the name when/if you publish it I would be eternally grateful.

Christian: I am probably not the most orthodox of believers but my faith is everything to me.

Sunni Muslim: Allah is the greatest.

Catholic: God bless ya.

Born Again Christian: Do you believe on the Lord God Jesus Christ as your Savior? Have you personally told Him you accept Him as your God and Savior? Romans 10:9 that if thou shalt confess with thy mouth the Lord Jesus, and shalt believe in thine heart that God hath raised him from the dead, thou shalt be saved. 10:10 for with the heart man believeth unto righteousness; and with the mouth confession is made unto salvation.

Anglo-Catholic: Born Jewish, raised Atheist. Converted two years ago. Still not baptized.

Buddhist: May you find peace, may you be at ease, and may you be free from suffering. And if that doesn't work, there's always pizza.

Bahá'í: Not sure of the purpose of this work you aren't pursuing, but if you require more information on the Baha'i faith or my personal view, you are free to contact me.

Atheist: I wish you the best of luck with your research.

Agnostic: You have excellent questions.

Chinese Buddhist with Taoist Leanings: :)

I don't have a religion: I am a gnostic atheist and apistevist. These questions assume too much about me but I felt the need to show a different perspective. We have no intrinsic purpose and objective morality is an oxymoron. You decide what is good and bad and why you bother continuing on living. If you want to matter you influence the life of those who come after you in whatever way you see fit. It doesn't matter in the end.

Taoist: These are really well crafted questions for dealing with a multitude of religious viewpoints. I hope you find what you're looking for!

Religious Society of Friends (Quaker): I have answered these questions from my perspective which is in unity with the original founders of Friends faith, who lived in the 17th century. Most Friends today are of the Liberal or Evangelical branch of Friends, and will have different perspectives. Yet, I believe that wherever people love and seek to come into the truth, the original Quaker faith can be rediscovered and once again formed into a People of God.

Agnostic Buddhist: I wish it wasn't so important to everyone to know where we came from, why we are here, and where we will go. I wish sight wasn't always the first thing we all use as judgement. I also, wish that more humans realized how much we are all the same. Is it really going to take us a global occurrence to see we are all one? It scares me to think of this... I wish everyone wasn't so focused on which religion is correct. We are all capable of making the right choices and having enough compassion to figure this out together. We need to make up our minds, religion is a personal journey for everyone. We will all find our own way through and it should never be anyone else's business or job to make everyone believe what they believe. I guess that is it, really. Thank you for giving me a chance to share my choices and journey.

Quaker (Christian): You are loved.

Taoist: A glance at the Tao Te Jing will give you a starter on Taoism. But, understand that it is only a text, not the text from which much of Taoism arises.

Jewish, mainly Reform: My faith brings me peace and happiness.

Daoist: Given that Daoism is often misused in the West, I hope there are not a lot of people answering with just "just go with the flow bro, Daoism is just like, chill out dude".

Open ended, minded: It is better to speak one-on-one in person than through media.

Eastern Orthodox: Glory to God!

Eastern Orthodox: Interesting book idea, but can be somewhat misleading in theory. A spiritual journey should be as much intellectual as spiritual. You should not be comparing what's different (different religions), but what might be right. Not just "what feels good spiritually". There's a lot of history and philosophy that should be taken into consideration.

Spiritual: Be one with yourself and others.

Undefined: Thank you for taking interest in the opinions of others. Cheers.

Taoist: You are beating around the bush. Eat three or four dried grams of magic mushrooms and then you'll know.

Buddhist with a splash of Christianity, Taoism and Raja Yoga: I may not have answered in line with other Buddhists. Some questions don't really have answers. Some questions aren't worth asking. Buddhism is quite different from other spiritualties. There is faith; but the faith is that your actions matter. :)

Muslim: These are some great questions you have here. Good luck with your work.

Buddhist: Have a nice day.

Sikh on paths of Sikhi: Guru as defined in Sikhi is 'the teacher who bring light to the darkness'. Guru Granth and Guru Panth are aspect which are the guides for Sikhs to connect to the Divine.

Jewish (Traditional/Orthodox): "I suggest you study the commentary".

Made in the USA
Middletown, DE
19 November 2020